HOW TO BABYSIT A LEOPARD

HOW TO BABYSIT
A LEOPARD

AND OTHER TRUE STORIES
FROM OUR TRAVELS ACROSS SIX CONTINENTS

TED & BETSY
LEWIN

A NEAL PORTER BOOK
ROARING BROOK PRESS
NEW YORK

To adventurers past, present, and future

Special thanks to Bill Kontzias for the still-life photography
and to Steve Cohen and Steve Klein for hosting our travel show at Pratt Library

Text copyright © 2014 by Ted and Betsy Lewin
A Neal Porter Book
Published by Roaring Brook Press
Roaring Brook Press is a division of Holtzbrinck Publishing Holdings Limited Partnership
175 Fifth Avenue, New York, New York 10010
mackids.com

Cataloging-in-Publication Data is on file at the Library of Congress

ISBN 978-1-59643-616-9

Roaring Brook Press books may be purchased for business or promotional use. For information
on bulk purchases please contact Macmillan Corporate and Premium Sales Department
at (800) 221-7945 x5442 or by email at specialmarkets@macmillan.com.

First edition 2015
Book design by Jennifer Browne
Printed in China by Toppan Leefung Printing Ltd., Dongguan City, Guangdong Province

1 3 5 7 9 10 8 6 4 2

CONTENTS

We Have Seen   1
"Guess What?"   5

AFRICA

It Begins   7
The Artist's Eye   11
A Penny for His Thoughts   12
Roger's Pan   14
The Sing   17
A Foreboding Place   19
Saffron Man   20
Tent Peg   21
The Gift   25
Window of Opportunity   26
Fort Portal   29
Lime Green Rubber Boots   30
Thirty Years of War   32
Gotta Go   33
Termitomyces   34
Mopani Worms   35
Night Leopard   36
Big Boy   37
Osama Bin Lion   39
Babysitters   41

ASIA PACIFIC

The Terai   43

Bruce the Mongoose   45

What Are We Doing?   46

Mahabil   47

Wrong Way   49

Sloth Bear   50

It's a Jungle Out There   51

Procession   53

Bloodsuckers   54

Snakes and Bats   55

What Was That?   58

The Artist   60

The Shaman   61

Mongolian Wrestling   64

EUROPE

Scrooge   67

Corrida   71

Feria   75

Noviada   77

Harry's Harbor Bazaar   78

The Hard Way   81

Gypsy Horses   84

The Bath   85

SOUTH AMERICA

Town Pier   87

The Englishman   89

Blue and Yellow   91

Rio Negro   92

The Plaza   93

Wild Horses   94

Giant Tortoise   95

The Standoff   96

Flying Underwater   98

The Consolation Prize   99

Jungle Walk   101

The Clay Eaters of Manu   102

THE UNITED STATES OF AMERICA

The Crater   105

The Captain and the Mongoose   108

Tit for Tat   109

Pretty Little Thing   110

Broadwing Kettle   111

Storm Front   112

Roadhouse   113

Homer Pigeon   115

Thirst   116

Squirrel   118

Pyramid Lake   119

Roundup   120

Amphibious Landing   123

The Pigeon   125

Car Service   126

Natural History   127

Pale Male   129

AND ONE MORE . . .

Mercy Flight   130

Index   133

Us in the
Okavango Delta,
Botswana

along the road. Equatorial sun is
getting to us. MURCH. FALLS Go on and suddenly
find ourselves the only bus left.
We dally, relishing our solitude.
Barb, Paul, Ted & Me. Basil is
patient as we lurch to a stop
everytime an ear flicks or a
wing spreads. This trip has been
full of unexpected little surprises
and we were treated to one as we
approached the bank of the Nile
across which lay Paara Lodge
A sort of ferry met us and
Basil drove the bus aboard.
All preferred to stand on the
ferry and dig the Nile. I tried my
best, but simply couldn't believe
I was really there. My effort was
interrupted by the head of a hippo—
salmon pink in the sunlight,
breaking the surface of the water

Journal pages

WE HAVE SEEN

We have seen some amazing things in our lives.

We have stepped out of a *lavu* at midnight 120 miles above the Arctic Circle at thirty degrees below zero and seen the shimmering green lights of the aurora borealis.

Cape Hunting dog
Okavango Delta

We have placed our hands on
the still-warm flank of a tiger killed
moments earlier by a rival tiger.

We have seen a pack of Cape hunting dogs
tear an impala fawn to bits in the blink of an eye.

We have seen a lone white wolf stampede a herd
of wood buffalo in the Northwest Territories.

We have seen thousands of pilgrims swarm
down the ghats in Beneres to bathe and
purify their souls in the sacred Ganges.

On Yellow Water Billabong we have seen a green
tree python slowly swallow another snake headfirst.

We have seen a scorpion spider
the size of a dinner plate on a night
walk in the Peruvian jungle.

plane ticket folder,
Mongolia

Betsy looking for her binoculars

From a *machan* high in a tree in Chitwan we have seen one-horned rhinos step out of the night forest looking like hammered silver in the moonlight.

In the Top End we have seen twenty-foot saltwater crocodiles, longer than our skiff.

We have watched thousands of puffins and gannets wheel overhead as our zodiac bobbed in the North Sea off the Westman Islands of Iceland.

We have seen hundreds of red-and-green macaws burst out of the rain forest on the Upper Mother of God River in Peru, carpeting the riverbank's salt lick in gorgeous colors.

Abdul Hoc

We have seen a storyteller in Fez toss a white dove high in the air and wait for it to come back with a story from the sky.

Mongolian plane ticket and journal page

Tomorrow we leave Ulaanbaatar with its *ger* "Suburbs" sprouting up the surrounding green mountain sides like white pillboxes. These suburbs grew like wildfire about the 1990s when people forced leave the countryside. Our guest a slight pretty mongolian girl named Batsuren "fearly Warrior" a

Us with the Masai, Tanzania

We have seen child jockeys race across the Gobi on half-wild Mongolian horses called *murs*.

By flashlight we have seen a leopard high in a tree gnawing on the skull of an impala with beautiful lyre-shaped horns.

We have felt the spray from Iguazu Falls in Brazil, the Victoria Falls in Zimbabwe, and the great Murchison Falls in Uganda as it roars through a twenty-foot-wide gap to become the Victoria Nile.

We have sat in a drenching rain watching a duck-billed platypus forage for food in the Rocky River on Kangaroo Island.

We have seen, from an elephant's back, a tiger kill a chital fawn and take it to her cubs hidden deep in the jungle.

We have seen mutton birds fresh from Siberia fall from the night sky all around us on Heron Island on the Great Barrier Reef.

Cape buffalo skull

Mongolian tent on wheels

passport

We have seen chimpanzees hunt, kill, and devour a red-tailed monkey in Kibale Forest in Uganda.

On the Siberian border of Mongolia, we have seen a reindeer shaman dance, and heard her speak in tongues.

We have seen blue-footed boobies and browed albatross with twelve-foot wingspans dance on Hood Island in the Galápagos.

We have seen a herd of reindeer in northern Norway race by us in the snow, sending up ice crystals tinted rose by the setting sun.

We have seen a deadly puff adder slither silently beside us as we sketched a hartebeest carcass in the Kalahari.

We have sat ten feet away from a five-hundred-pound silverback mountain gorilla in the Impenetrable Forest of Uganda.

There are still so many things to see . . . like the ancient city of Petra carved out of solid stone or Kazaks hunting with golden eagles or maybe even . . . starships off Venus.

Ted sketching
Aran Camp
Kharakhorum
9/5/04

Have camera case, will travel!

"GUESS WHAT?"

Our whole life of travel started in a phone booth.

Our first date confirmed that we were meant for each other. We loved the same movies, had the same sense of humor, and loved animals. All Ted had to do was show me photos of his pet lion cub and chimpanzee, and I was hooked.

The biggest dream we shared was to travel to East Africa to see the great herds of the Serengeti before they disappeared altogether. Since we were just married and short on cash, it didn't seem to be within our reach.

One day I was walking down Madison Avenue and happened to look up at a big sign on the side of a building that read ADVENTURE TRAVEL.

I decided it was a good omen so, heart pounding, I found myself climbing the stairs to their second-floor offices. An hour later I found myself in a phone booth calling Ted.

"Guess what?" I said. "We're going to Africa!"

Finally, the childhood dream of a little girl from Clearfield, Pennsylvania, and a little boy three hundred miles away in Buffalo, New York, was about to come true.

Our big adventure to East Africa was to set the tenor of our lives. We saw herds of wildebeests a million strong on the Serengeti Plain. We saw black rhinos, elephants, lions, leopards, giant forest hogs, and gorgeous birds like carmine bee-eaters, lilac-breasted rollers, and forest kingfishers that light up the sky like fireworks. We saw tens of thousands of flamingos feeding in the Ngorongoro Crater, and the famous tree-climbing lions of Manyara. We visited nearby Olduvai Gorge where the skull of Lucy, the oldest humanoid in the world, was discovered.

Some Africans told us then, "You should have seen this in the 1950s."

This was 1970. The last time we were there was in Uganda in 1997. They said, "We wish you could have seen this in the 1970s."

We had.

Sketching in the Serengeti

Rissani

Cairo

Kibali Nat. Pk.

Bwindi

Tree Tops

Serengeti

Okavango

Kalahari

N
W E
S

AFRICA

IT BEGINS

Africa! We couldn't believe we were actually on our way. We took pictures of each other on the plane, grinning foolishly.

Before we knew what hit us we were in a safari van looking at herds of wildebeests and zebras a million strong, thundering across the Serengeti Plain. We saw a cheetah mom chirp to her cubs, then go into overdrive at sixty miles an hour after a Thompson's gazelle. We saw a rare black rhino napping in the

Rhino
Ngorongoro 1990

Joseph Ildefonsi
Land Rover
Ngorongoro
Crater

Hand woven Botswana bracelets

Ngorongoro Crater, and the tree-climbing lions at Lake Manyara. We saw magnificent
Masai warriors, called Marons, and women mantled in beautiful beadwork. We stayed
up all night at the Tree Tops Lodge waiting for a giant forest hog to appear at the water

Masai

Hartebeests Hornala Kat

Amboseli

hole. The next morning we were mugged by a troupe of olive baboons led by a female named Gertrude with a tiny baby clinging to her. We saved our cameras and binoculars, but they got our breakfast.

At the end of our journey a fellow traveler about the age we are now said to us, "You will always have these memories. No one can take them from you."

No one ever has.

Zulu jewelry

THE ARTIST'S EYE

Ted: One day on a game drive just outside Nairobi we came upon a grazing antelope with lyre-shaped horns called a topi. We stood up in the van for a better view from the roof hatch. The sun shone on its mostly gray coat. As the topi raised its head, its neck and back turned to a kaleidoscope of color.

"Look at the gorgeous pinks and lavenders, and the golden glow," I said.

"I see purples, and tinges of blue and copper," said Betsy.

There was a couple standing next to us. I heard the wife whisper to her husband, "Are they looking at the same animal we are?"

Tree Tops Lodge, Kenya

A PENNY FOR HIS THOUGHTS

Kalahari, Botswana, May 1981

Ted: In the blackness of the Kalahari night, Ebonine, a bushman, squats at the edge of our roaring camelthorn fire puffing deeply on his bone pipe and staring into the flames. Sid, my old friend and guide, stands with me near the crest of a high dune overlooking Xangua Pan, watching a bloodred moon slowly rise above the horizon. As jackals on the pan began to yip and wail, I turn from the moon to look at Ebonine in the soft light of the fire. "A penny for your thoughts," I think. I ask Sid to ask Ebonine what he's thinking. Sid calls him over. Ebonine is so tiny standing next to us in his blue coveralls two sizes too big and a jackal fur cap. I ask Sid to ask Ebonine what he finds most beautiful about the Kalahari.

Ebonine in his jackal fur hat

Sid questions him softly in Tswana, a language they both understand. I look from one face to the other as the conversation goes back and forth. The word *Ghanzi* keeps popping up. Ebbe (as Sid calls him) says it, and Sid shakes his head no.

"What does he find most beautiful?" I ask.

"Nothing."

"Nothing?" I say.

"Nothing," says Sid. "He finds nothing beautiful about the Kalahari. It's too hard here. What he does find beautiful is going to Ghanzi. It's where he met his wife, and where he thinks he will find work."

Ebbe's head turned at the familiar word *Ghanzi*.

"I won't say his name so he won't know I'm talking about him. He has no idea of the situation in Ghanzi. It's a cattle station four hundred kilometers to the west of here.

There are seven thousand bushmen there, all looking for occasional work. The locals pay them less than a pula a month to tend their cattle out in the bush. The cattle, as you've seen, denude the land making it unfit for game. There is nothing for them to trap or hunt. They are starving. So one of them occasionally kills a steer. They get seven years in the slammer for that. It's bloody awful there."

Ebbe is staring out over the pan in the direction of Ghanzi, unaware of what we're saying, or what the future holds for him.

"Ask him about his family," I say.

"Ebbe says he has two children, one tiny, one about seven. They don't understand numbers, so it's hard to find out exactly how old they are. The boy is as old as the last big rain."

Ebbe says something, his voice now more relaxed and intimate. He's touched by us wanting to know more about him and his family. He tells Sid he will take us to meet his family tomorrow.

"Ask him if his son will learn to snare and hunt and find the sipping wells." At this question Ebbe's voice becomes vehement. He stands straighter, and touches his chest with the palm of his hand as he talks.

"He's taught the old ways to his son," says Sid. "His seven-year-old has gone into the bush alone many times. He can make snares to catch birds, traps for animals, he can hunt with a bow he made himself, and can make fire by rubbing sticks together. He can find the sipping wells and knows how to make sipping straws. He knows how to carry water in an ostrich eggshell, and find a dozen different kinds of roots and tubers."

When Sid stops speaking there is silence. Ebonine leaves, slides another log into the fire, squats down, and is lost again in his thoughts.

ROGER'S PAN

Kalahari, Botswana, May 1981

Stray donkeys dot the pan, a dry depression in the land with a hard surface of mineral salts. Women, bundles on their heads, babies on their backs, walk slowly toward the smoke haze on a far dune. A cart drawn by four donkeys brings up the rear. It's a crude wooden affair with fat rubber auto tires. The village is a drab collection of beehive-shaped huts, like boils on the side of the dune, enveloped in a blue smoke haze.

Roger's camp

In the village there is an overwhelming sense of hopelessness. The bushmen have been drawn here by the easy access to water at the nearby mineral exploration camp. They grow a few melons, and the men still go out on hunting forays, but they are tied to this camp by the water. They have always found water or moisture in this harsh desert, as have the animals, but the twentieth century has now brought it to them. It's changed them. They take occasional labor for wages in the camp. There is not much left to hunt in the area. They've been here too long.

Starving dogs roam the village compound. "This is Ebonine's village," says Sid.

"I found Ebbe at Xangua Pan about six years ago. His wife, an old lady, perhaps his mother, and

14

a small child were with him. He was living in the bush as he always had. This is now his village."

Some of the bushmen are quite tall with golden-tinged skin. Some have Bantu features. One fellow wears black western clothes, and a five-gallon hat, a Kalahari cowboy. He

leans on his donkey, resting his head on folded arms atop a handmade leather saddle. His broad smile reveals brown stumps of teeth.

Inside a ten-foot *boma* of grotesquely twisted branches with no roof is Ebbe's family. His wife is Lilliputian, with golden skin and delicate bushman features. She is nursing an elfin newborn, their second. Sid tells us she will not leave the *boma* until the baby has reached the prescribed age. She finishes nursing, and hands the baby to an old woman with no face who squats next to her.

Ebonine with his wife and baby

15

The old woman has a piece of rough burlap wrapped around her head and covering her absent face. Open sores mar her forehead, and there is a deep hole where there once was an eye. She is a leper. She scurries crablike to the other side of the *boma*, and turns her non-face toward it.

Finding water here in the Kalahari Desert, an area devoid of surface water, taking everything they need from the land, never more than they need, was their way of life. What does having more water than they need do to their souls? Yet, how can the camp deny them water? But to give it to them will destroy them in the end. In this place their souls will die of thirst.

Ebonine's wife with the woman with leprosy

THE SING

MOTH COCOONS

Kalahari, Botswana, May 1981

Ted: The bushmen begin arriving in small groups as the sun sets. They just appear out of the bush. They don't use the sand track where they would be safer from the bite of the puff adder. They sit in a circle around the fire, women with babies astride their backs. As they sit they unwrap the babies and swing them around to the front and the warmth of the fire. One of the children begins to cry. Pistolo, the chief, lifts it up and holds it up to the night sky. He points at the billions of stars and the Milky Way. The child sucks his thumb and is quiet, enchanted by the heavens.

Gathering firewood

One woman begins a chilling wail and a rhythmic hand clap. Other women join in. The dancing begins. The men stand up and begin stamping their feet in cadence with the clapping of the women. Puffs of sand are thrown into the air by the force of their stamping feet. The wailing and clapping get louder. One fellow wears a moth cocoon rattle on his ankle. They begin to imitate animals. An elephant. From the darkness into the glow of the fire comes the rope maker. He has an old sneaker dangling from his mouth, an improvised trunk. We can see an elephant. It moves toward the wailing women, then backs off into the dark. The dance ends with a whoop and much laughter. The wailing resumes. Next comes a strutting ostrich. The fat babies stare in wonder at the flapping, whirling bird, parading in and out of the light.

At last the dancers are spent. Sid steps into the firelight and tells them that we thank them and respect them. The women wrap their babies in their blankets and, as the fire dies, they all melt into the night.

A FOREBODING PLACE

Kalahari, Botswana, May 1981

It was tough four-wheel driving all through the lonely, rugged, and very remote Ngwezumba Molapo Valley. The map shows an earthen dam that was built in 1970 to help retain water for game. The walls of the river gorge are twenty feet high. Only pools of water can be seen as we approach the dam, now overgrown with rank grass. On the ridge above us, wild seringas splash the yellow of their fall colors, and fat-trunked baobabs glory in their brief burst of leaf. The place feels as though no one had looked at it for a very long time.

Three Cape hunting dogs materialize at the far end of the dam. One squats in a bush to mark it. Sid parks the cruiser and we walk slowly toward them out onto the dam. The dogs cross a sandbar to the opposite bank, and with backward glances, climb up its steep sides.

We are distracted from them by a strange sound coming to us from the pond below. We look over at the pond and see the carcass of a dead animal. There is a lot of splashing and a strange sucking noise. We move closer. It's a gruesome spectacle. Twenty feet below us is the headless corpse of a kudu, a large antelope with spiral horns, half-submerged in the water.

"It's a lion kill," says Sid. "I can see the deep tear wounds on its flanks." One whole shoulder is gone. Inside its belly and chest cavity, which rest in the water, are five enormous catfish, writhing and wriggling like living entrails. They tear and suck at the flesh. They lift their silver bodies half out of the water as they push and shove for the best spot. Their ugly, wedge-shaped, bewhiskered heads appear, mouths agape. They grab chunks of flesh, and thrash frantically. As they worry the flesh, they make obscene slurping and sucking sounds. It is both fascinating and revolting. They have at the carcass for fifteen minutes, then almost as one, they slide out of its belly and sink below the surface.

Suddenly, our legs turn to fire. We are covered with stinging fire ants. We beat them off, and retreat from this foreboding place.

SAFFRON MAN

Taroudant, Morocco, December 1994

On the road to Taroudant, in an area known the world over for growing saffron, the spice that gives such pungent flavor and deep orange color to food. It is very precious as it comes from the stigma of the crocus flower and is picked by hand. There was a tiny roadside shop in the middle of these vast fields of flowers where a man was selling the saffron.

We went into his dark little shop with our guide, Brahim. The turbaned saffron man nodded, and offered us mint tea poured from a silver pot into tiny glasses.

Through Brahim we asked the price of the saffron.

"Fifteen dollars," said Brahim. Fifteen dollars a pound? We thought that was really cheap. At home it costs a fortune for a tiny glass vial. We told Brahim, "Tell him we'll take four pounds." The saffron seller's eyes really lit up, and he replaced the tiny balance scale on his counter with a larger one. He carefully poured a large pile of the saffron onto the scale and checked the weight.

"Fifteen dollars a pound is really cheap," we told Brahim.

"It's fifteen dollars an ounce," said Brahim. He spoke to the saffron seller whose face wilted as he carefully poured the saffron back into its jar.

"We'll take an ounce, please."

TENT PEG

Rissani, Morocco, December 1994

Ted: I told Abdul Hoc that I was not interested in buying a tent peg. I don't own a tent. Especially one that needs a three-foot-long carved wooden tent peg.

"It is the tent peg of my people," he said proudly.

outside Maison Tuareg

A few hours earlier we had asked Brahim, our Arab driver, "Will we get to see the blue men?" They are the fabled Tuaregs. In the old days they would lie in wait in the desert to attack the last unsuspecting member of a camel caravan, then rob and perhaps kill their victim. Of course, that was a long, long time ago.

"So you want to meet a blue man," said Brahim, eyeing us in the rearview mirror with a mischievous grin. Two hours later we pulled up in front of a mud-walled shop on a narrow street in the town of Rissani. Above the door hung a pair of antelope horns, and a sign that read Maison Tuareg. Out came Abdul Hoc, grinning broadly, and his brother, Abdul Rocman. They were dressed in the indigo-dyed blue caftans and turbans of the blue men.

"I'll leave you to it, then," said Brahim with the same mischievous grin, and left us.

"Welcome," said Abdul Hoc. He ushered us inside and asked us to remove our shoes. It was dark and cool. The walls were covered in Berber rugs. Tile work glinted on the floor. There were trunks of silver and amber jewelry, colorful horse blankets, jewel-encrusted scimitars, antique fusils decorated with ivory and silver, ceremonial saddles, and carved tent pegs by the dozens.

Donkey saddlebag

"Now, what can I show you?" asked Abdul Hoc. I said I was interested in saddle blankets and was whisked out of the room by Abdul Rocman, leaving Betsy to the mercy of Abdul Hoc. It was the old divide and conquer trick.

I selected a donkey saddlebag from the dozens hanging from the ceiling, even though I don't have a donkey. When I returned to Betsy, she was sitting cross-legged on a Berber rug with Abdul Hoc surrounded by trunks full of antique Tuareg jewelry spilling over the top, and glass cases on the wall crammed with bracelets and necklaces of silver. It looked like Ali Baba's cave. Betsy picked a necklace strung with paper-thin silver balls and big amber stones. "How much?" I asked. Abdul Hoc invited me to join them on the rug and called for tea. Then the age-old bargaining began. As we sipped our tea, he jotted something on a piece of paper and handed it to me. I noticed for the first time that his hands were smooth as silk. He'd never done a day's work in his life. He had written $250 on the paper. I crossed it off and wrote $125 underneath it. He took a sip of tea, wrote, and handed the paper back to me. He had crossed off my offer and written $250 again. This went on. Each time I raised my offer a little, he crossed it off and wrote $250. Apparently he had not read the same guide book as I because he was supposed to settle somewhere in the middle of our first offers. I finally relented and agreed to $250. Now we were ready to leave and pay for our items. "You must see some rugs," said Abdul Hoc. "We already bought rugs in Fez," we said. "But, you haven't seen *my* rugs," he said. He led us to the inner sanctum of the place, an enormous room piled to the ceiling with rugs—huge rugs that would fill a ballroom and tiny rugs the color of saffron. He spread out a Berber rug on the floor, dropped to his hands and knees, and began a

Inside Maison Tuareg

The tent peg! →

masterful performance piece. "There are three kinds of weaving in Berber rugs. Look here, embroidery, and here it is knotted, and here, woven. There are symbols woven into the fabric by Berber women." He pointed at a design on the rug. "This is a river, and over here is a village." As he pointed, he scurried on his hands and knees, arranging his long blue caftan as he went. This went on for a long while, and he was perspiring profusely. He finally stood up and said, "These are the rugs of my people," and leaned exhausted against the wall.

"Now," he asked, "which one would you like?"

"None, thank you," we answered. "We already bought rugs in Fez."

Chagrinned, but not beaten, he said, "How about a tent peg?"

So now here we were discussing a tent peg that I didn't want.

"What would you offer if you did want it?" he asked.

"But I *don't* want it," I answered.

"Say you did want it. What would you pay?"

By now he had me in the corner, and Betsy had been whisked away again. I wondered where my shoes were.

"$25," I said.

"You insult me! This is the tent peg of my people. I will give it to you for $75."

I said, "That's a good price but I'm not interested."

"Make me another offer," he said.

Now he had me *bargaining* for something I didn't want. "$35," I said, hoping he wouldn't take the offer.

"Look at the intricate carving and beautiful design. $75."

"$45," I said. I still didn't want it.

"You know, not only is this a tent peg, it is also a sundial."

"I don't need a sundial. I have a watch."

"But, it is the tent peg of my people."

I said, "I don't have that much cash."

"No problem," he said as he pulled a credit-card machine from the folds of his blue robes.

THE GIFT

The next day Brahim brought us the message that Abdul Hoc wished to give us a gift. Brahim seemed very impressed by this offer. We weren't so sure. The day before we left, our arms laden with our treasures, and my three-foot-long tent peg/sundial, Abdul Hoc had reached out and filched a pen from my shirt pocket, then a box of film from my vest pocket. They disappeared among the folds of his blue robe.

His gift was a generous one, a Land Rover with a driver and Abdul Hoc's brother, Abdul Rocman. They wrapped our heads like theirs with yards of indigo blue fabric. Then we were off into the wondrous walled villages, called *ksors*, and the lush date palm oasis. Then we drove deep into the black rock desert where every stone you pick up bears the fossil of an ancient sea creature.

Rock with fossils of sea creatures

Betsy: As Abdul Rocman led us through the narrow, palm-lined lanes of the *ksors*, we were joined by a passel of children all screaming, *"Stilo! Stilo!"* (Pen!) with outstretched, expectant palms. Abdul Rocman waved them off with angry shouts, *"Ishmay! Ishmay!"* (Go away!) More children arrived, and screamed even louder *"STILO! STILO!!"* I told Abdul Rocman that I had some chewing gum. Could I give it to them? Maybe they would go away. He nodded. The children formed a circle around me with their palms extended. I put a stick of gum into each little hand. When I reached the end of the circle there was a great big hand. I looked up. It belonged to Abdul Rocman.

WINDOW OF OPPORTUNITY

Bwindi Impenetrable Forest, Uganda, December 1997

Things had been quiet for a while so we decided to take this window of opportunity and go. We'd been planning a journey to see the mountain gorillas for five years, but things kept happening. First the civil war in Rwanda, then unrest next door in the Congo. We had heard of a group of mountain gorillas in a place called Bwindi Impenetrable Forest in Uganda, but Uganda was having its own war in the north. We called the American embassy in Kampala. "You didn't hear it from us, but I wouldn't go to Bwindi myself," said the voice on the other end of the phone.

But now it all seemed to have quieted down, not counting the two hundred and fifty thousand refugees, and an outbreak of cholera in Goma just fifteen miles south of Bwindi. We finalized our plans for a car, driver, and guide with an African company to be paid in advance in U.S. dollars, cash. They assured us it was safe. When we landed in the airport in Kampala our guide, Delores, rushed up to us and embraced us. "You're here, at long last!"

That night we waited nervously with pockets full of cash in a seedy little hotel on a back street. The rep from the company showed up, never looked at us, which made us very uneasy, took the money, counted it quickly, and left. The next morning Delores showed up with a van and driver and we headed for the back country. Thirty miles from town the tarmac ran out, and red mud tracks took over. The countryside was beaten

Gorilla permit

Kacupira, silverback of K Group

Betsy on a slope with porters

and bruised from years of civil war. We slid and skidded in the muck, got bogged down more than once but finally, nine hours later, arrived at the lantern-lit African Pearl Cottages in Bwindi. That night as we stowed our gear and readied for bed, we couldn't help discussing what would be the best escape route if there was any kind of trouble. Maybe we would slip out the back door of the cottage and hide in the dense jungle.

The next morning Delores handed us over to a Bwindi guide and told us our trek would be three hours at most. As we headed up the mountain, we passed guards with automatic weapons. "They are there to protect the gorillas from poachers," our guide was quick to say.

Nine muddy, exhausting hours later we had just about given up on ever seeing gorillas when our guide said, "The gorillas. They are just there." We could see the vegetation moving, but we couldn't see them at all. We could hear their grunts. It sounded like people clearing their throats. We moved closer through knee-deep nettles tearing at our legs. Our guide reached out and pulled back a tangled *Brillantaisia* vine like a curtain, and there, all five hundred magnificent pounds of him, sat Kacupira, the silverback leader of this group. He was stuffing stems and leaves in his mouth. We were

Kacupira
yawning

just ten feet from him. He ignored us completely. We watched him until our allotted hour was up, and we began the trek back in the near dark.

Altogether it had been twelve brutal, exhausting hours. We staggered back into camp in the pitch black, covered in mud from slipping and sliding on the treacherous volcanic slopes, soaked with sweat, and shivering violently in the night chill. Delores rushed forward and threw her arms around us. "I've never been so glad to see anyone in all my life!" she cried. It was as if we had returned from the dead.

"We're filthy," we said.

"I don't care. I'm just so glad to see you. Thank God you're okay."

We told her the gorillas, once we found them, were awesome, but the trek was brutal, the tangled forest was impossible to walk in.

That night we couldn't get her extreme relief at seeing us out of our minds. After all, we were only trekking to see the mountain gorillas. What could happen?

Two years later Hutu rebels from the Congo came down the mountain and attacked the camps at Bwindi, including the African Pearl Cottages, shot the guards dead, singled out Americans, kidnapped them, took their shoes, and force marched them up the mountain toward the Congo. Those who couldn't make it were killed. Some escaped. When she heard the first gunshots, one girl slipped out the back of her tent and hid in the dense jungle.

FORT PORTAL

Fort Portal, Uganda, 1997

Ted: "But, sir, why are you leaving us early?" asked the desk clerk at the Mountains of the Moon Hotel. I told him that we needed to be near the Kibale Forest where the chimpanzees were. It was not safe to drive after dark, and it was too far away to be there early in the morning, the best time to see the chimps. What I didn't tell him was that the bullet and mortar holes in the hotel walls bothered me. The thousand-yard stare of the people in the nearby market bothered me, that we were the only guests in the hotel bothered me, the thunderstorm in the hills the night before that sounded like mortars bothered me. Thinking about the dense evergreen trees in the hotel compound as a possible hiding place if we heard the sound of automatic weapons bothered me. And, the old man guarding the place with the useless, single-barreled shotgun and the pathetic watchdog on a leash really bothered me.

So, we packed up and left with our guide and driver, heading for the Crater Lake Hotel near Kibale. The hotel was six round, thatched huts called rondavels on the slope of the volcano's crater overlooking the lake. At the entrance to the hotel, an old man wearing an army greatcoat opened the gate and we drove through it. The odd thing was there were no walls on either side of the gate. We could have just driven around it.

That evening I mentioned my anxieties about the Mountains of the Moon Hotel to the manager. Her eyes glazed over. "Things are quiet . . . for the moment," she said. The last part of that sentence bothered me. We went to bed that night in a pitch-black rondavel with a shriek of frog sounds that made sleep impossible. At first light I looked up toward the front gate without walls. There, silhouetted against the sky, was the old man in the greatcoat. He was standing guard with a bow and arrow.

Ted by a big
fig tree

29

LIME GREEN RUBBER BOOTS

Kasanai, Uganda, December 1997

All day long on the way to Queen Elizabeth National Park we passed jeeps full of Ugandan combat troops armed to the teeth with automatic weapons. We stopped for tea in a little roadside shop and picked up a local newspaper. It said that the rebels had distributed flyers saying they were going to attack the airstrip in Kasese, our lunch stop today. We had wanted to have lunch in the bush somewhere to keep a low profile, but Delores said not to worry. She wanted us to have lunch at a small hotel she knew.

The hotel was up on a hill, and had a patio surrounded by a low stone wall with a view of the whole town below, and the mountains all around, the same mountains where the rebels were hiding. We sat exposed on the patio having our lunch with the odd feeling that someone might be looking at us through a sniper scope.

Suddenly we heard vehicles pull up below, car doors slamming, and men yelling. We looked down over the low stone wall. There were a dozen jeeps with combat soldiers leaping out of them. Delores said calmly, "I think we should leave now."

We started down the stairs just as the soldiers started up. They all carried automatic weapons, wore camouflage, green berets, and lime green rubber jungle boots. Their faces were grim, their eyes hard. As they rammed past us into the hotel, Betsy came face-to-face with the captain, a huge man with the hardest eyes of all. "Hello," she said sweetly, as if we were meeting a neighbor on our morning walk. He shouldered past her into the hotel with the rest, and they began kicking down doors.

The next day we picked up another newspaper. It said units of the army had attacked a rebel group in the mountains above Kasese, and they had killed its leader. They knew it was he because he was wearing a long white scarf.

Betsy: We left Bwindi and were on our way to Queen Elizabeth National Park. As we rode along in our combi my eyes scanned the mountains. "That's where the rebels are," I thought. "I wonder if they're watching us with binoculars." We were still jittery after our guide Delores's extreme relief when we returned to camp so late after visiting the gorillas, and from the lady at Crater Lake Hotel saying, "Things are quiet . . . for the moment." The jeeps full of combat soldiers that kept passing us didn't help either.

We had been warned about the possibility of fallen trees or other debris that would cause us to stop the vehicle and try to clear the road. It could be a trap. We could be ambushed by rebels hiding in the roadside brush who would rob, and perhaps even kill us.

At last we stopped for lunch at a small hotel above Kasese. Sitting at a table on an

← The boots!

open patio, and still keeping a wary eye on the mountains, we heard the screech of brakes, slamming car doors, and gruff, muffled voices. We jumped up and ran to the steps where I nearly collided with a soldier the size of a refrigerator in camouflage, a green beret, and green jungle boots. He glared at me, stone-faced.

"Hello," I said, smiling weakly. He shoved past me like I wasn't there, and he joined the rest of the troops in batting down the doors in the hotel.

31

THIRTY YEARS OF WAR

Uganda, 1997

Ted: We had been driving for hours. The Mountains of the Moon rose up on our left, and to our right as far as the eye could see, African savanna. The last time we drove this track was nearly twenty-seven years ago. Then it was teeming with animals: elephants, giraffes, zebras, impalas. Now it was empty, devoid of any living thing. We finally came to the Kazinga Channel where, amazingly, the same boat and boatman from twenty-seven years ago was waiting to take us upriver to Murchison Falls where all of Lake Edward empties out through a narrow twenty-foot gap.

Twenty-seven years earlier the shores were thick with hippos, and lined with crocs more than twenty feet long, the biggest in the world. There were still hippos, but not so many, and the biggest crocs were a mere ten or twelve feet. The beautiful lodge overlooking the channel, once brimming with visitors, was reduced to rubble by mortars and machine guns. This is what thirty years of civil war has done. Marauding armies killing elephants for ivory, shooting hippos and crocs for target practice and game out on the savanna to feed their starving soldiers.

Now here we were, the *only* guests in the brand-new lodge, sitting in the cavernous dining room, being served by a dozen waiters and a world-class chef. Thirty years of civil war.

GOTTA GO

Xakanaxa Camp, Okavango Delta, Botswana, April 1999 and December 2007

Betsy: It's not easy going to the bathroom in the bush. You run into all kinds of problems. At Xakanaxa Camp in the Okavango Delta, Botswana, if you have to go in the night you must leave the safety of your tent and walk a hundred feet to the outhouse, or loo, as they say. "Watch out for the hippo," we were warned. "You have to sweep your flashlight back and forth in front of you and check the bush on both sides. If you see a pair of shining eyes and a wall of wet flesh, put something between you and it." Meanwhile, you still have to go, and the loo is still fifty feet away. If you do make it there without a hippo, there's the leopard to worry about on the way back. Of course, when the hippo's gotta go, he just splatters it all over your tent with his flicking tail.

The loo!

Ted: One time in the early evening I was in the loo already when the hippo decided to make an appearance. He hauled himself out of the river and began grazing right outside the loo. The loo is made of reeds and branches. If he leaned on it, it would fall over. At least this happened after I had done my business, so I just sat there on the toilet to wait it out.

33

TERMITOMYCES

Xakanaxa Camp, Okavango Delta, Botswana, February 1999

With the rain come the mushrooms. They grow only on the huge termite mounds that dot the landscape like medieval battlements. Their scientific name is *Termitomyces*, but the local Tswana people call them *mabua*. We had passed a termite mound just outside camp, a big one about fifteen feet high. It was early morning, and the forest was wet with last night's rainfall. There were no mushrooms then, but the next morning the mound was bursting with white mushrooms the size of pizzas. They had very long, slender taproots that draw nutrients from within the mound. As we picked them, we stepped very carefully so as not to crush new mushrooms just pushing like fists through the surface. We filled the back of the land cruiser with them. They were full of beetles and other insects. Washed free of the insects and peeled, they are wonderful to eat.

Later on we saw a huge termite mound covered not with mushrooms but with birds. Glossy starlings, red-billed and yellow-billed hornbills, and helmeted shrikes all feasting on termites as they crawled out of their holes to fly. The rain makes mushrooms grow and termites fly. Nearby, yet another mound, this one covered with mushrooms and a troupe of chacma baboons. They were pulling up mushrooms, gorging on them, and eating the termites as fast as they appeared. In five minutes all the mushrooms were gone.

Our guide Sheila
and our guide Arabang

MOPANI WORMS

Xakanaxa Camp, Okavango Delta, Botswana, April 1999

The local Tswana people who work in Xakanaxa Camp love to eat Mopani worms. It's their favorite snack. They also eat them in a stew with their traditional mealy meal. They harvest them twice a year, handpicking the big, brightly colored caterpillars or shaking them out of their host Mopani trees. They pull off their heads, then squeeze the bodies to remove the bright green guts. Then they are cooked in salty water and dried in the hot African sun. They have three times more protein than beef, and the fattest ones are said to have the best flavor. We have visited this camp many times, and luckily have avoided the Mopani season.

"Too bad you just missed Mopani season," they'd say, or "Too bad it's not yet Mopani season."

We always acted disappointed, though secretly relieved that we didn't have to swallow big, fat, green caterpillars. The last time we visited the camp our luck ran out.

"You're in luck! We saved some Mopani worms for you."

A big bowl was brought and set down in front of us. Then they all stood around, eager to see our reaction. We looked down at the bowl. They were gray and slimy, just laying there. All we could think about were the green guts that had been squeezed out of them. We each gingerly picked one up, and popped it in. It slid down tasting like slippery, fishy, salty popcorn. They all nodded their approval. We gamely swallowed another.

"Mmmmmm, delicious," we lied. "We'll save the rest for later."

That night in our tent by lantern light we read about Mopani worms in our field guide, picking away at the bowl of worms as if they were popcorn. They went down a lot easier in the dark when you couldn't see them.

Footnote: If not harvested, Mopani worms will leave the trees and pupate underground. Then a beautiful Emperor Moth will emerge from the pupa, mate, and lay eggs in the Mopani tree completing the cycle.

Yuk!

NIGHT LEOPARD

Xakanaxa Camp, Okavango Delta, Botswana, December 2001

We are driving back to camp in the pitch black with our guide, Ali. We are late leaving the Moremi Reserve. All vehicles are to be out of the reserve by 7:00 p.m. We were detained by a pack of wild dogs on the hunt. "They will understand," says Ali. "You don't often see wild dogs, especially hunting."

A hippo appears in our headlights. He's as big as our truck. He turns, and runs for the safety of a nearby pond. Ali stops the truck by a big jackalberry tree. We hear hyenas yipping in the blackness of the surrounding forest. Ali holds a hand to his ear. "Listen!" We listen. Then we hear it, the cracking and crunching of teeth on bone. Ali smiles broadly. "Good," he says. "She's back on the kill." We pull up underneath the tree, the crunching quite loud now. Ali plugs his big floodlight into the dashboard and turns it on. In the beam, a blaze of orange with black spots lights up the night, and a pair of luminous yellow eyes throws the light back at us. Ali says, "It's three days old. I thought she had abandoned it."

The leopard is twenty feet up in the fork of the tree with the remains of an impala buck. She had horsed it straight up the trunk where it would be safe from hyenas, jackals, and lions. She is gnawing on the skull, its beautiful, lyre-shaped horns still attached. The strong spotlight cast on this grisly scene makes it strangely theatrical. She ignores the light, now gnawing on a leg bone, finally getting at the brilliant red marrow. Her long tail hangs down behind her, invisible in the black night except for the white tuft at the end of it.

A side-striped jackal patrols the base of the tree waiting for any scrap that might fall to the ground. A baboon barks in the forest.

Ali looks at us with a sly smile. "Now we are really late, but they will understand. It's not often you see a leopard, especially up a tree on a kill."

BIG BOY

Xakanaxa Camp, Okavango Delta, Botswana, December 2001

The old man walked through camp at dusk hanging oil lanterns on poles every six feet or so along the paths. They would light the way to your tent in the dark. We sat by the fire circle and watched him, then turned to watch the sun fall into the delta, and the sky become brilliant with stars. We caught the low-water pond smell of the big resident croc as he hauled himself up onto the riverbank. In the distance we heard the resident hippo grunting.

We stared into the crackling fire. Suddenly, we noticed that some of the lanterns had gone out. Then, miraculously they relit on the left as others went out on the right. Something big was moving between us and the lanterns, blocking the lights as it went. Two long, curved shapes, eerily white in the starlight, solved the puzzle . . . a bull elephant, the biggest we'd ever seen. He made no sound, this black shape, as he moved forward, extinguishing then relighting lanterns. He walked past the kitchen compound where there was a cluster of lanterns allowing us to see his silhouette clearly.

We had been told about him. "Big Boy," they called him. He was on a mission, on his way to a fruiting marula tree at the far end of camp. He'd been coming to that tree to feast on his favorite fruit long before the camp was here. Rod, the camp manager and a third-generation African, pulled up a chair next to us by the fire and lit his pipe. "Something, isn't he?" he said. "Biggest we ever saw," we replied. Rod said that for two nights

Big Boy blocking the lights

At Hippo Pools

now he has not been able to get to his tent because the marula tree is right next to it and Big Boy is blocking his way. "What do you do?" we asked.

"I talk to him about all kinds of things," he said. "The other night I even gently pushed his tusk away from my deck railing so he wouldn't smash it. And he obliged. I'm just not afraid of elephants."

He told us that Big Boy was heavy in musth. This is when elephants secrete a fluid from glands in their temples at a certain time each year and become very aggressive. As we talked, Big Boy appeared by the lights near the kitchen.

Rod got up without a word and walked toward him. We ran behind a tree. Rod walked right up to Big Boy and shined a flashlight on him. He was huge, and Rod looked puny next to him. There was white showing in Big Boy's eyes. He drew up to his full height of twelve feet, spread his ears, and trumpeted. Rod stood his ground not ten feet away. Then Big Boy lowered his head, and shook his huge ears violently. Incredibly, Rod held up his hand and said in a soft voice, "Please stop. There's no need for this. Just go about your business." Big Boy stopped dead in his tracks, turned, and ambled off into the dark, putting out lanterns with his bulk as he went. Then all the lanterns were lit, and he was gone.

Rod came back to the fire, relit his pipe, and said, almost apologetically, "I'm just not afraid of elephants."

Rod and Big Boy

38

OSAMA BIN LION

Xakanaxa Camp, Okavango Delta, Botswana, May 2007

Our driver, Ali, saw the lion two hundred feet away and stopped the vehicle. "Can we get closer?" we asked. "Not with *that* lion," he said. "We were out gathering firewood when he jumped right on the trailer and tried to leap in the truck with us. I don't get anywhere near that one."

"What's his name?" we asked.

"He doesn't have a name. He just showed up here recently."

"We've got it! How about Osama Bin Lion?" Ali liked it.

The next day we spotted Osama lying in a thicket with several lionesses. We watched from a good distance for a while as he dozed. A call came over the radio that our truck was needed in camp as it was the only one with a winch. Another truck would be sent and we could switch. Ali drove some distance away from Osama, and met the other

uh, oh!

truck. We all got out, talking and laughing and standing around. Ali looked over our shoulders and said, "We'd better get back in the vehicle." Osama had stood up, and was glaring at us.

As we drove away, the other driver yelled to Ali, "Watch the clutch. It slips once in a while, and it might stall."

We headed back toward Osama who was now rigid and staring at us with glowing yellow eyes. Then, for some reason, instead of driving sideways, Ali drove directly up to him and stopped. Osama roared and charged, covering the distance between us in a split second. Ali tried to start the truck. The clutch slipped. It stalled. Osama was alongside the truck. We ducked and cringed, waiting for his sharp claws and teeth. Finally the truck started, wheels spinning, and we lurched forward. Osama stayed with us. He roared as he looked for a way to get into the open vehicle. Ali banged his hand on the door to distract him. He kept coming. Ali swerved around trees and crashed through thickets, with Osama in hot pursuit. Finally we reached open ground and the truck sped ahead. Osama broke off the chase at the edge of the forest. His sides heaved, his tongue lolled, and his eyes burned yellow with fury.

No one knows where he came from, or why he behaved the way he did. Maybe, they said, he came from an area where hunting is allowed and had been shot at. He disappeared the next day, never to be seen again.

BABYSITTERS

Xakanaxa Camp, Okavango Delta, Botswana, May 2007

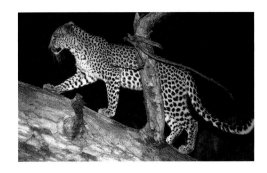

She was as sleek and graceful as a ballerina as she tiptoed along the branch of a huge jackalberry tree. Then she lay down, back legs straddling the branch. She peeked demurely at us through the leaves. Our driver told us this leopard cub was six months old. He said when she was tiny, her mother kept her hidden from visitors, but one day unexpectedly and to everyone's delight, she appeared carrying the cub in her mouth for everyone to see. Ever since then she seemed to feel comfortable leaving the cub in the care of onlookers while she went hunting. Now she was hunting. "So we're the babysitters?" we said to our driver.

The cub climbed fearlessly up into the topmost branches, then leaped from one branch to another as we gasped at her derring-do. Then, she settled down to nap.

That evening she lay stretched out on the lowest branch as regal as the Queen of Sheba, then paraded back and forth in the light of our torch like a model on the runway, as elegant a creature as we had ever seen. Then she leaped twenty feet straight up into the leafy tree canopy, her show over for the night.

The next morning she was gone. How forlorn the tree seemed without her. Our guide read their footprints called pugmarks in the sand. First the mother's coming in, then the cub's joining hers, then walking away together on their way to feast on her kill.

The Queen of Sheba

41

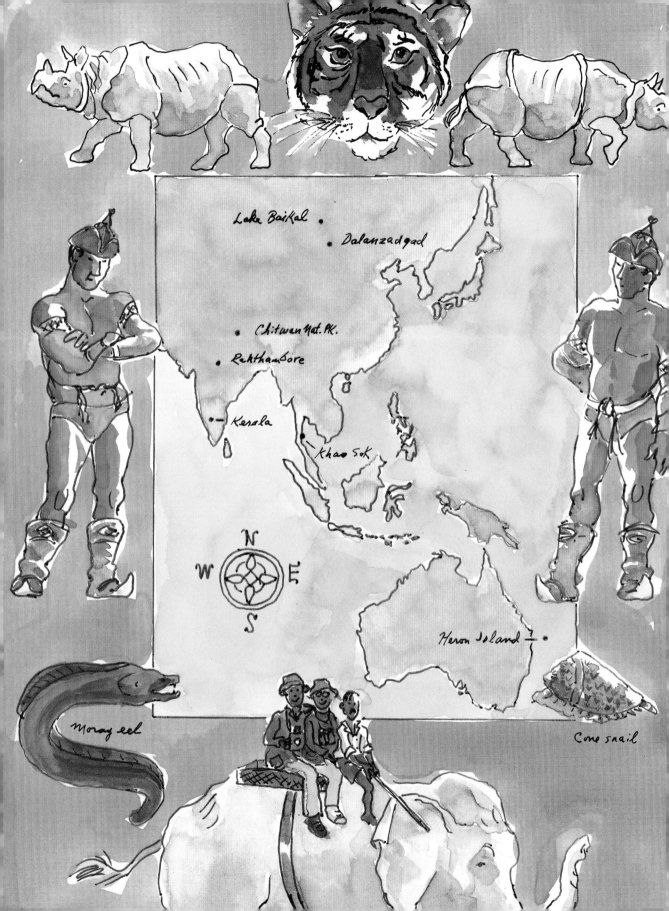

Lake Baikal

Dalanzadgad

Chitwan Nat. Pk.

Ranthambore

Kerala

Khao Sok

Heron Island

Moray eel

Cone snail

ASIA PACIFIC

THE TERAI

Nepal, February 1983

A dozen women wearing colorful saris sat in the middle of the mountain road breaking large rocks into smaller ones, then they passed them on to other women who made them smaller yet. And on it went until they had made gravel to build more roads. The road stretched from Kathmandu, down the foothills of the Himalayas, to the Terai, a jungle area along the Nepalese border with India.

Along the way we passed pilgrims carrying a corpse wrapped in a white sheet splattered with red dye, like blood. They were taking the deceased to Pashupatinath to be cremated, the ashes to be scattered upon the sacred Bagmati River. They carried the corpse slung between long shoulder poles with a jaunty, almost festive air.

We drove across a shallow river. People were being ferried across in dugout canoes. One man stood in the bow of an overcrowded canoe with his bicycle. The trees along the riverbank had been pruned so severely by local villagers for forage for their animals that they looked like an alien species.

❃❃❃❃

It was late afternoon when the elephant arrived, a big tusker owned by the Nepalese government. We climbed a ladder and crawled into the howdah. A big metal thermos of hot tea was loaded on with us. The mahout urged the huge beast forward with little kicks behind its ears. Soon we crossed the Dungla River into Chitwan National Park. The sun

Betsy and friend

was leaving quickly as we crossed the tall grass, and was gone completely from the jungle.

Across a clearing in the jungle, high in an old kapok tree was a *machan*, an elevated platform originally used for tiger hunting. We were to spend the night here. We entered the platform through a trapdoor in its floor, the mahout handed us the hot tea, and we pulled up the trapdoor. We watched the elephant slowly, silently melt into the darkening jungle. We were alone. We wrapped ourselves in our sleeping bags, drank some tea, and waited.

A bright moon rose above the trees, bathing the clearing beneath us in soft silver light. We had begun to nod off when we heard the snapping of twigs, and the scraping and rustling of branches in the jungle. Out of the black shadows into the silver light came three one-horned rhinos. Their thick, armored plating looked as if it were made of hammered silver. They stopped and sniffed the air in the middle of the clearing, shaggy ears alert. They seemed to be expecting something, but then they slowly moved off and were swallowed by the inky darkness.

We curled up in our sleeping bags, glad for them against the night chill, and closed our eyes. We both dreamed of silver one-horned rhinos.

Rhinos at dawn

BRUCE THE MONGOOSE

Guida Camp, Chitwan National Park, Nepal, February 1983

Ted: "Look, a mongoose!" said Betsy.

We were sitting by the Dungla River at Guida Camp. The mongoose scooted directly toward us.

"Don't worry," said the camp manager. "That's Bruce. He hangs around the camp. He's okay."

Bruce came over to Betsy, crawled into her lap, then draped himself over her shoulder. Betsy was enchanted. She hugged him and kissed him on the head. "Look how sweet he is," she said.

Later that day we saw Bruce rooting in a pile of elephant poop to get at the partially digested kapok seeds.

A new friend

Kiss! Kiss!

WHAT ARE WE DOING?

Guida Camp, Chitwan National Park, Nepal, February 1983

We were walking along a jungle trail near Chitwan National Park when our guide suddenly yelled "SLOTH BEAR!" and took off after it through the tall grass.

We took off after the guide. We caught a glimpse of an unkempt, furry black shape crashing through the grass ahead of us. It was running for all it was worth. So were we. We were trying to catch up with it. We stopped abruptly, gasping for air.

"A SLOTH BEAR? Are we crazy?"

A picture we had both seen in a magazine when we were kids flashed into our minds. It was of a villager whose face had been raked off by a sloth bear. They injure more people than tigers do, in some places. When they attack, they go for the face with a swipe of their awesome, three-inch-long claws. They can also bite, clinging like a bulldog.

"What the heck are we doing chasing one?"

MAHABIL

Ranthambore, Rajasthan, India, February 1983

Ted: You have to know that Mahabil did not speak English, and the rest will follow. We had told the night clerk in the hotel in Delhi that we needed a car and driver for the next morning. We were heading for Jaipur, called "the pink city" for the color of its buildings, Ranthambore to see tigers, and the Taj Mahal in Agra. The night clerk handed us a card and told us that these people were Sikhs and very honest.

The next morning we went to the location written on the card. Their office was a huge wooden packing crate standing on its end on the street corner. It had travel posters stuck to the walls and a folding chair. We told the turbaned man sitting in that chair that we needed a car and an English-speaking driver for ten days. "No problem," he said.

Two hours later Mahabil showed up at our hotel. He leaped out of the big, black, Indian-made Ambassador car, ran around to open the door for us, and saluted. He was as thick as a fireplug, had a neck like a bull, and wore the obligatory silver bracelet that all Punjabi men wear. He was dressed in a crisp, light blue shirt and pants. He smiled as he closed the door, and off we went. It took less than two minutes to realize that he spoke no English. From then on it was sign language.

Mahabil

After a while we got thirsty and made a sign that meant drinking. He pulled up to a little stand on the street where we bought six bottles of Taj Mahal beer. When we got back to the car, Mahabil reached for one of the bottles. I drew back, but he grabbed the neck of the bottle. I pulled. He pulled. I looked at his face. It was angry. "I'm not going to let him drink beer while he's driving," I thought. With one last pull he snatched the bottle away from me. Boy, was he strong! Then he reached over, and with the bracelet on his wrist

neatly popped off the cap. Then, smiling sweetly, he handed the open bottle back to me.

He drove all the way to Ranthambore with the horn blaring at holy cows, rickshaws, camel caravans, and trucks. When we finally arrived, our host, Fateh Singh, said, "Send your driver away. You won't need him. You can take the train from here on. It's better." Mahabil stood there at attention and smiling, oblivious to everything that was being said. "We can't send him away," we said. "We made a deal with the Sikhs, and they are very honest people. So we're going to need a place for him to stay while we're here."

Fateh Singh waved it off, saying he would be fine on his own for the week, and we shouldn't worry about him. Then he told Mahabil in Hindi to pick us up a week later. So off he went in the big, black Ambassador that was now covered in thick, red dust.

That night Fateh Singh invited us to sit by his fire. He clapped his hands, and out came his houseboy in the traditional dress of Jaisalmer, Fateh's hometown. He sat cross-legged by the fire, and began playing two flutes at once from each side of his mouth while Fateh sang a wild folk song. When he translated the song into English our laughter melted into the inky black jungle around us.

After a week of watching tigers stalk through the ruins of a maharaja's palace, charge into the lake after sambar deer, and spray on our open jeep at arm's length away, it was time to bid farewell.

Mahabil showed up on the button, spiffy in his freshly pressed uniform, the Ambassador now gleaming in the sunlight. We wondered how he had fared on his own. We didn't have to wonder for long. We drove to the nearby town of Sawai Madhopur where he had stayed the week. Mahabil turned onto the main street, driving very slowly. The people poured out of their shops and houses and lined the street six deep. They all began cheering. As the car proceeded slowly along, Mahabil nodded beneficently, waving his hand to the people, like the pope. Fateh Singh was right. He did just fine on his own.

Fateh Singh

WRONG WAY

Kanha National Park, India, February 1983

Ted: Just outside of Khana National Park we were staying in a rondavel with a thatched roof and walls that boasted of an interior toilet. The toilet was a hole in the ground with blocks of concrete shaped like human feet on either side of it to show you which way to face while squatting. If you faced the wrong way you missed.

I was using it one evening, facing the right way when, from the rondavel next door, I heard a man's voice exclaim loudly, "OH, MY GOD!!"

He should have looked at his feet.

Wrong!

SLOTH BEAR

India, February 1983

The road was hot, dusty, and jammed with traffic. Huge trucks laden with gravel roared by. The landscape all around was used up, desolate. Alongside the road was a man with a bear. It was a half-grown sloth bear. It stood on its hind legs and hugged the man around his waist. At our approach the man held up a rope that laced through the bear's pierced cheeks and nose. He raised a long staff over the bear's head. The bear began to dance.

Sloth bears live deep in the forest. They eat fruit, honey, and flowers, and are especially fond of ants and termites. They vacuum them up with special lips and a concave palate. They blow into the nest, then suck up the ants with closed nostrils to prevent the angry ants from going up their noses. They can suck up to ten thousand termites at a sitting. They love the flowers of the Mahwa tree. When the flowers ferment they are full of alcohol. The local people think they make the bears drunk causing them to dance.

Paw prints and dung found along cliff edges suggest that the bears sit there to enjoy the panoramic view of the forest below. Mother sloth bears carry their young cubs on their backs as they search for food. Rural villagers believe the bear is the protector of little children . . . this bear dances on the dusty road to Delhi.

IT'S A JUNGLE OUT THERE

Heron Island, Australia, October 1986

Ted: Almost everything out there on the reef either stings or bites or, for that matter, could eat you. It's a jungle out there.

There are starfish out there that can grip a clam, pull it open, throw up its stomach into the clam, digest it, then draw its stomach back in through its mouth.

There are snails out there that can extend their necks and send microscopic barbs into you like miniature whalers' harpoons. A half hour later you go blind, then you can't speak, then you die. A lady once took one home to add to her shell collection. A week later she took it from the shelf to polish it. A half hour later she went blind, and you know the rest.

Sea cucumbers are another story. If you pick one up it squirts water out its front end

Sea cucumber

. . . I think it's the front end. Then if you squeeze it a little and get it mad, it'll lay out this long viscous drool-like substance. If you *really* get it mad, it'll disembowel itself, dumping its insides into your lap. It saves the outer skin for a new set of insides to grow in. Another kind of cucumber secretes a substance that sand sticks to so it looks like the sand it's laying on. If you pick it up and rub off the sand your hands will be dyed a deep red color.

There's a fish called a butterfly cod with venomous spines all over it. It can cause severe reactions in humans, such as intense throbbing pain, blistering, vomiting, paralysis of the limbs, and sometimes heart failure. It sure is pretty. I'll say that for it.

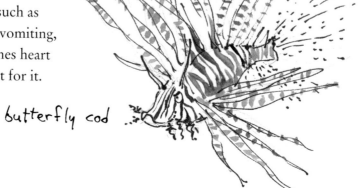

butterfly cod

blue-ringed octopus

There is an octopus with bright blue rings all over it, not surprisingly called a blue-ringed octopus, that people can't resist picking up. It's the last thing they'll ever do. Its venom will cause you to become nauseated, go blind, and be unable to speak or swallow. What's really awful is that you're completely aware of what's happening to you. Then you die. There's no antidote for the venom, and the octopus secretes enough poison to kill twenty-five humans in minutes.

Then there's the giant clam. It filters its food, taking in water through a hole on one side and dispersing it through a hole on the other. Also, if it gets mad it'll squirt water right in your face. It can't eat you, but if you stick your finger in between the top and bottom shells they SLAM shut! Think about it.

There are brittle stars out there that, rather than getting eaten, will give up an arm or two. It's okay, though. They can grow them back.

There are moray eels, too. Tiny ones, big ones. They have very sharp front teeth. When they grab something with those teeth they withdraw into their holes in the coral. Their teeth slant backward, so if it's your finger it's withdrawn with, and you try to pull it out, it'll shred it to the bone.

One tiny little crab dresses up like a dandy, decorating itself with bits of surrounding vegetation and shells. Its unfortunate prey must feel like it's being eaten by the landscape.

There's a snail out there that will crawl up on the back of another snail, and scrape away with its rasp-like tongue until it's drilled a hole through the shell. Then it slowly eats its prey.

There's a big, *really* big white worm that lives under the coral. It secretes a sticky slime all over itself that gets caked with sand, making a revolting envelope for the worm to live in. Then, from under the coral, it sends out dozens of foot-long white feelers that it controls like fingers to feed on minute organisms in the water. If it gets upset, or loses its sand shell, it simply breaks itself in half.

I never heard of so much stinging, vomiting, disemboweling, crushing, secreting, and shredding, and I haven't even mentioned the things that can eat *you*!

It's a jungle out there.

PROCESSION

Ooty, India, January 1997

We had just ducked out of the rain into a little tea shop in Ooty, a hill station in Tamil Nadu, when the clang of cymbals and wild chanting drew us outside again. At the end of the narrow street was an enormous elephant wearing a gold-studded face plate with six priests riding on its back. They held umbrellas and shields covered with gold coins, fans, and goat-hair fly whisks. Twenty men wearing black headbands surrounded the elephant chanting wildly and clapping their hands. Children ran through the crowds with big brass boxes, begging offerings.

The elephant's front legs were shackled to its hind legs with heavy chains that rattled as the elephant shuffled along. The sound of those heavy chains stayed with us for days.

BLOODSUCKERS

Kerala, India, January 1997

We were in the Biligiri Hill Station north of Mysore, the name taken from the exposed white limestone hills thereabouts. We were driving with our guide, Suni, and a ranger armed with a shotgun against wild beasts should we decide to take a hike in the jungle.

Gun bearer!

We came to an enchanted place, a lovely crystal-clear stream bubbling from a spring that rippled over the rocky bed. We asked if we could stop and explore the place. Suni seemed reluctant but finally said okay. The ranger with the shotgun went on alert. We got out, set our jackets on a rock, and wandered around the edge of the streambed. It was an exceptionally beautiful place.

Suddenly, we became aware that the ground all around us was moving . . . *crawling*. We looked closer. The leaf cover, ground, and water were solid with leeches on the move, inching and humping toward us. There was blood to suck, and they knew it. We grabbed our coats, and leaped into the rover. "Gaghh! That was awful," we said. Suni shook his head apologetically. "I was afraid of this. Shake out your coats and check under your pants!"

We picked up our coats. They were crawling with two-inch-long black leeches. We beat them off, then lifted our pant legs, hands shaking. Attached to our legs, swollen now to twice their size with our blood, were a dozen leeches. We began pulling them off in a panic, blood streaming down our legs from the wounds where they had attached themselves. We worked feverishly, as it was unbearable looking at them sucking away like that. Finally rid of them, we calmed down. We looked at the ranger with his shotgun. The look on his face said, "If it had been a tiger I could have done something."

Leeches are skinny before they eat.

SNAKES AND BATS

Khao Sok National Park, Thailand, March 2000

Floating huts, Khao Sok

Ted: It was early morning, Khao Sok National Park, Thailand. The gibbons were swinging wildly through the trees, and their haunting hoot songs echoed off the sheer limestone cliffs and across the lake.

We were in a long-tailed boat so named for its long rudder, with Tom, our guide, and a few friends. He motioned the boatman to turn into a small jungle stream. "About a mile up this stream we'll leave the boat and hike up to the cave," said Tom. He had told us the night before about this cave. It was famous for being the last holdout of the antigovernment forces years ago during the civil war. It was so well fortified that no one would venture in there, not the government soldiers or the loggers, and so the forest remained intact. It's also the home of the bat-eating snake, which is the main reason we came.

"When we get to the cave we'll hike in. Then we'll have to swim for a while, finally holding our breath and diving underwater to a hidden chamber. All of this in the pitch black," said Tom.

The boat finally came to a stop, bobbing up and down in its own wake. Tom jumped onto the slippery, rocky shore, and held the line. Betsy stepped to the bow of the boat and jumped. As if in a slow-motion dream, I saw her right foot tangled in the handle of a duffel that had been stuffed under the

Oops!

Ted shooting at floating market

gunnel. Then she was gone over the side. I heard a sharp cry. I looked over the side of the boat at a horrifying scene. Betsy was hanging upside down by one foot, like an animal caught in a snare. She was bobbing up and down with the motion of the boat, her head inches from the rocks. The foot caught in the snare was facing the wrong way. I jumped out of the boat, and helped Tom and the boatman lift her and disentangle her foot. I said stupidly, "Are you all right?" She answered very calmly, "No."

Tom leaped into action. "It's dislocated, and probably broken." He gave her two aspirin and instructed the boatman to take us back across the lake to get help. The sun was up now, and beating down fiercely. Two friends offered to go with us. It was a three-hour trip back across the lake to the dam that years ago created it.

We rigged a sunshade for Betsy, who began to sing, as she always does when she's upset. We all joined in to sing "Button Up Your Overcoat." Odd choice considering that it was about ninety-eight degrees. The boatman looked at us quizzically.

When we reached the dam there wasn't a soul around. There was a huge flight of stairs leading to the road. We carried Betsy up fireman-style. Now we were on a deserted jungle road. We waited. By now Betsy was in shock. "It doesn't hurt," she insisted. Finally, an old pickup truck came by. We flagged it down, and with sign language (none of us spoke Thai) we showed them the situation. We understood their sign language immediately. One man rubbed his thumb and forefinger together, the universal gesture for money. So we fed him bills until he nodded yes.

We lifted Betsy gently into the truck bed and climbed up next to her. Two bumpy hours later we came to a village where there was a clinic. We carried her past

a few scrawny chickens into the waiting room full of sick children and old people. Amazingly, there was an X-ray machine, and it confirmed Tom's diagnosis. We were told Betsy needed surgery, and they gave her some painkillers. We called the hospital in Phuket on the other side of the country. It was the only one in the area. We asked the surgeon to wait for us. We hired a van and driver, and put Betsy in the backseat where she promptly fell asleep. Four hours later we pulled up to a brand-new hospital with the surgeon and three nurses, in starched white uniforms, waiting in front with a gurney. The minute I saw them I knew we were in good hands. We said farewell to our friends and thanked them.

In the hospital they readied Betsy for surgery and off she went to the operating room, singing softly to herself.

They had to screw a metal plate onto the bone so it would knit properly and, of course, turn her foot the right way around where it belonged. The surgeon came to Betsy's room the next day to have his picture taken with her for his album.

Three days and much therapy later, we were in an ambulance on our way to the airport. When we arrived, there were dozens of fresh-faced kids with backpacks just off the plane, eager for their Thailand adventures. The nurses opened the back of the ambulance and lowered Betsy down on the gurney. Betsy held her arm across her eyes to block the sun. The backpackers' mouths fell open.

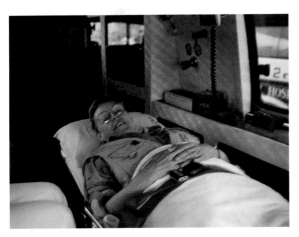

Smile, Betsy!!

"Betsy," I whispered, "put your arm down and smile. They think you're in agony. You're scaring the daylights out of them."

When we got home we made an appointment with an orthopedist to continue Betsy's care. He looked at the X-rays and declared it a perfect job, and that not many hospitals anywhere in the world had the equipment to do this kind of procedure. Most of all he admired the stitches. "I want to take those out personally so I know how it was done," he said.

Months later Betsy said, "You know I'm really sorry we missed the bat-eating snakes, but I'm *not* sorry we missed diving underwater in the pitch black to that hidden chamber."

WHAT WAS THAT?

Three Camel Lodge, Mongolia, July 2004

Betsy: We were staying in the Gobi in a big, round nomad tent called a ger.

A swirling cloud of insects, big ones, little ones, were drawn to the lights above our beds. We watched them dreamily until we felt sleepy, then doused the lights. Immediately, they all rained down on us, tic, tic, tic, tic, onto our blankets, our faces, into our eyes and ears and noses like a thousand tiny pebbles. We sputtered and swatted, and flapped the blankets until they all disappeared.

Betsy in ger wearing a head lamp

I was just falling asleep when I heard a shuffling sound. "What's that?" I whispered to Ted.

"I don't know. Sounds like someone shuffling around in bedroom slippers."

I was almost afraid to shine a flashlight on the intruder, but I did. The slippered intruder turned out to be a huge cricket the size of a cucumber shuffling across the floor. I shut off the flashlight and sank back on my pillow.

"I hope he sleeps with Ted, not me," I thought.

I had a similar experience when I awoke suddenly in our cottage at The Cock of the Rock Lodge high up in the cloud forest of Peru to a crunching sound and a familiar aroma.

"What are you eating?" I whispered to Ted in the dark.

"Nothing. I thought *you* were eating something," he said.

"Well, *somebody's* eating something," I said. "It smells like an apple."

I remembered stashing one under the nightstand between our cots. I fumbled for a

58

No slippers!

flashlight and shined it where the apple was. It was still there, at least the core was. We fell back asleep confident that whoever or whatever ate the apple was not looking to eat us.

The next morning we asked our guide, Monika, if she had any idea who the culprit was.

"Probably a 'possum," she said.

"How did it get in there?" I asked.

"It was probably already in there," she said.

I wondered what else might be already in there.

And yet another time I had just fallen asleep in our cottage at the Manu River Lodge in Peru.

Tap, tap. Tap, tap, tap. Tap, tap, tap. I awoke with a start. From my cot in the dark I could just make out the open door to the bathroom where the tapping was coming from.

Knockety knock. Tippy tap. It was rhythmic, like someone dancing.

"Ted, are you awake?" I whispered.

"Yeah, what are you doing?" he asked in an annoyed tone.

"I'm not doing anything. There's someone or some*thing* in the bathroom."

"Go to sleep, Betsy."

I was pretty sure it wasn't the deadly fer-de-lance whose bite meant instant death, or an anaconda that could crush the life out of me. I also ruled out a wild javelina boar with slashing tusks. My curiosity got the best of me. Flashlight in hand I crept in the dark to the bathroom door, and quickly flashed the light on.

There on the shelf above the sink was a little cane rat grappling with a tube of toothpaste twice his size. He had managed to stand it upright in his effort to remove the cap, and was hugging it. Rat and tube twirled in the flashlight beam like dancers on a stage, the bottom of the tube tapping rhythmically on the glass shelf. I crept to bed.

"What was it?" asked Ted.

"Oh, just a cane rat dancing with our toothpaste tube."

"Go to sleep, Betsy."

THE ARTIST

Ulaanbaatar, Mongolia, July 2004

Betsy: I huffed and puffed in the high altitude as I climbed the hundred steps to the memorial overlooking the city of Ulaanbaatar. In the memorial was an eternal flame celebrating the lasting friendship between Russia and Mongolia. It was out.

A man carrying a portfolio stepped forward. He was wearing a fedora and a green silk *dheel* with a yellow *bus* around his waist. He opened his mouth slightly and what came out of it was astounding. First came the sound of bagpipes in the distance, then, a high-pitched, nasal sound like a flute. Then the twanging sound of a Jew's harp to the rhythm of horses' hoofbeats. As all this was going on, out came a very deep bass voice, then a different, higher-pitched voice. To top it all off came the sound of chirping birds. All of these sounds blended into a beautiful, harmonious song. I looked at my guide in astonishment.

"Throat singing," she said, chuckling. "He's an artist. He wants to show you his work."

He opened his portfolio. I bought a silhouette cutout of a horse and foal.

THE SHAMAN

Lake Baikal, Mongolia, July 2004

We sat in a tight circle in the *uurtz*, a tepee-like canvas tent. It was ten thirty at night and still light spilled in through the opening at the top. The stove had been kept burning all day long in preparation for the ceremony. It was like a sweat lodge inside. Outside, smoky fires bathed the dozing reindeer keeping away the tormenting flies and mosquitoes.

The shaman's husband, our guide, Batsuren, told us we must not leave the *uurtz* after the ceremony began and it would last two hours. We were sitting there waiting for the stars to appear. He went outside to look at the sky. He came back in shaking his head. "Not yet." The shaman sat on the ground smoking a fat hand-rolled cigarette, her high-cheeked face softly glowing in the light of one flickering candle. She looked composed and detached. The light outside began to fade. The shaman's husband threw open the tent flap and went outside to look at the sky. He came back in shaking his head. "Not yet."

carved
wooden
Bactrian camels

The heat was unbearable. The shaman's twelve-year-old daughter with a sloe eye was feeding juniper branches into the fire. It got darker outside. The shaman's husband looked again and nodded okay as he closed the flap. The stars were shining. The shaman stood. Her husband removed her traditional cape from its hook on the tent wall and placed the heavy garment on her shoulders. It was layer upon layer of strips of colored cloth overlapping each other. Their daughter thrust more juniper branches into the stove. They immediately burst into flame. She withdrew them and blew them out. They gave off a thick, pungent smoke. She waved them around her mother. Next she flicked reindeer milk from a bowl into the air with a reindeer antler. She did this repeatedly as her mother was being dressed. Next came the headdress. In the dim candlelight it seemed to be a black-horned hood with a veil of dark fringe covering her face. She was now only a shapeless, moving force.

More smoke and reindeer milk filled the air. The husband took a large, round skin drum that was hanging on the wall and placed it over the stove. The heat stretched the skin tighter, and he adjusted the tension until the sound was right. He handed it to her, then firmly took hold of her cape just under her arms. More smoke and reindeer milk. She began to beat the drum with a piece of reindeer antler. The sound of a slow heartbeat. She began to chant. Then her voice changed, emitting strange, unearthly sounds. She jolted violently as if shocked by electricity. Her husband held her tightly. She slumped, then jolted again. Strange wails and moans came from under the dark veil. The drumming went faster and faster, louder and louder. The smoke got

the antlers

thicker and thicker. Our hearts thump-thumped with the insistent drumming. She lurched toward us until she towered over us beating the drum, ba BOOM, ba BOOM. Suddenly she threw the antler three times into each of our laps.

Each time her daughter yelled *"Taruch!"* (Fortune!) when the antler landed the right way. Once, it landed wrong. The daughter was silent. The shaman threw the antler a fourth time and the daughter yelled *"Taruch!"*

Then her husband guided the shaman to her place in front of the stove and took the drum from her. He removed her cloak and she slumped to the floor in a trance. The daughter rifled in the dark for her mother's *haartsug* (traditional hat) and placed it on her head.

Enkhtuya Oudgan

shaman

sketch from Ted's journal

The shaman began to revive. Her husband handed her a freshly rolled cigarette and lit it for her. She took a long drag and drank reindeer milk tea from a bowl.

We sat in silence listening to the crackling fire, moved by what we had just witnessed. We waited for her to speak. She stared at the candle. Her face floated like a mask in a void of darkness. She turned and looked at us. She spoke softly and our guide translated simultaneously.

"I have seen all the spirits and all the gods. I've seen them very clearly. There are no obstacles. I see no obstacles in your future." She smiled sweetly. Then, "Whether you believe in shamanism or even understand what it is, is not important. What is important is that you were here tonight." She handed us each a small packet of juniper wrapped in muslin. She told us to light it and walk three times clockwise around our house. It would protect us.

She looked back at the candle and took another drag on her cigarette.

Reluctant to leave, we sat awhile longer looking at the candle with her. Then we thanked her in Mongolian: *"Bailla."* She smiled at our bad pronunciation and wished us a safe journey.

The tent flap dropped behind us as we stepped outside into the chill night air. The reindeer dozed in a stand of larch. Their fires smoldered. The sky was brilliant with stars, the very same stars our shaman had just returned from.

MONGOLIAN WRESTLING

Dalanzadgad, Mongolia, July 2004

janjin

"**M**ongolian wrestlers are national heroes," said our guide, Batsuren, as we sat on the ground in a big open field in Dalanzadgad, a little town in the Gobi. "Only men participate, unlike the archery and horse-racing events, which include females. Our greatest wrestler bears the title Invincible Titan."

In front of us, six burly wrestlers flapped their arms gracefully as they performed the "falcon dance." They circled their seconds as their formal titles and accomplishments blared over the PA to stir up their fans and unnerve their opponents. Other wrestlers waited their turns by a brightly colored tent set up at the edge of the field.

The wrestlers wore colorful leather boots with upturned toes called *gutals*, short red-and-blue silk jackets called *zodogs*, and brief trunks. They removed their *janjins* (generals' hats) and handed them to their seconds. Then they slammed into each other, grabbing the shirts and trunks of their opponent for leverage. Their faces turned scarlet with exertion as they pushed and shoved one another looking for an advantage.

Carved
wooden
wrestler

Their seconds circled, constantly encouraging them. Some contests were over in a few seconds. Others ground on and on in the punishing heat. There was no time limit. Finally there were only two wrestlers left, one short and stocky like a fireplug, the other six foot five and lean as a Southern preacher. They locked on to each other and strained for ten minutes. The tall one finally threw his opponent to the ground and stood triumphantly over him. The crowd cheered wildly. Then the loser passed under the winner's raised arm as a traditional gesture of respect.

As we watched them don their *janjins* and strut off the field, we said to Batsuren, "Funny, their shirts have no fronts—just sleeves and a back. Why is that?"

"A long time ago," she said, "a lady wrestler disguised as a man won the tournament, only revealing herself as a woman after her victory. Ever since then the shirts have been frontless."

Looking at these huge, hulking men we thought, "That must have been *some* woman."

65

EUROPE

SCROOGE

County Mayo, Ireland, August 1974

Day 1: they took us around to the stable on the Marquis of Sligo's estate to show us our horse.

"There he is," said the stable hand in a lilting Irish brogue. "His name is Scrooge. He'll be yours for the five days. Just one thing to remember, he's mad for the road."

Scrooge was huge and looked pretty much like all the other horses except he had a big wart on his nose. As the stable hand got the tack together we asked him, "How do you make him go forward?"

"Go on," he said.

"How do you make him go backward?"

"Go back."

With that sorted out we were shown how to harness him and back him into the shafts of our tinker wagon. We were given a big bag of "nuts" (horse feed), and we were sent on our way for five days through the Irish countryside in County Galway.

"How do we know where to go?" we asked as we pulled away.

"The horse knows."

The tinker wagon was a big orange plastic copy of the traditional wagons of the Irish Gypsies, or tinkers, as they are called. It had beds, a table with benches, and a stove. Before we could say "go on," Scrooge was trotting jauntily toward the front gates of the estate. The gate opening

Betsy with Scrooge

67

On the road, Killary Harbor

looked much narrower than our wagon. "The horse knows" echoed in our minds so we closed our eyes, and when we opened them the gates were behind us.

We were going along fine until Scrooge saw another wagon down the road in front of us. He took off at a fast trot. We tried to slow him down to no avail.

He came up behind the slow-moving wagon, and to our horror, started to pass it. The road was one lane wide, and it had steep berms on both sides. We pulled hard on the reins. No way! The people on the other wagon screamed at us, "What are you doing? Are you crazy?"

The wagons bumped each other, and ours tipped precariously on the berm. Scrooge kept going, passing the other wagon. The other people were now shaking their fists at us.

"Sorry!" we yelled. "It's the horse."

Scrooge saw open road ahead and finally slowed to a walk. I guess that's what they meant when they said he's mad for the road.

We were supposed to stop at a designated farmhouse after a few hours and spend the night. Scrooge was supposed to know where it was. We didn't. We came to a fork in the road. Scrooge took the left one, which was just wide enough for the wagon. We went along fine until a car appeared, coming the other way. The car stopped. Scrooge stopped. A young girl got out of the car and said, "You're not supposed to be on this road. Back the pony up."

"That's easy," we thought. We got down from the wagon and grabbed Scrooge's halter.

"Go back." Nothing.

"GO BACK!" Nothing.

"GO BACK!" Nothing.

Scrooge had a look on his face like "What?" The girl shook her head in disgust, grabbed Scrooge's halter, said very quietly but with an Irish accent, "Go back."

Scrooge got all mushy and backed all the way down the road to the fork. So much for the horse knowing the way.

We headed toward the sea on the right fork, and when we got to a cottage Scrooge stopped.

"Go on," we said. Nothing.

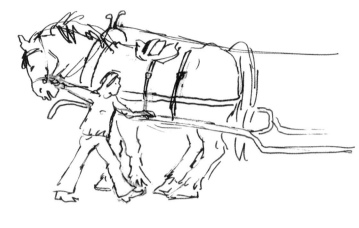

Go back !!

A farmer came out to welcome us with fresh bread and eggs. We unharnessed Scrooge and put him to pasture. Early the next morning as we went along the strand to get him, a fox appeared on the rocky shore. He was so beautiful in that morning light that we stopped dead in our tracks. He was gone in the blink of an eye.

Day 2: We arrived at Dew Loch, unhitched Scrooge, and walked him a mile down the road to a fenced-in pasture. The next morning we awoke to pouring rain and a big traffic jam on this lonely back road. There, about a hundred yards down the road, was Scrooge. No doubt about it. We saw the big wart on his nose. There was no room for the cars to pass, and he wouldn't budge. He'd broken the fence and headed for our wagon because he wanted his nuts . . . now! We finally lured him off the road with his bag of nuts. Then just because it was pouring rain, Scrooge completely forgot how to back into the shafts. He went sideways and got them between his legs, and kept tripping on them. When we were thoroughly soaked, he decided to cooperate.

Day 3: We parked the wagon at Croh Patrick and set Scrooge free in the pasture. He immediately headed up the mountain. The next morning, nuts in one hand, halter hid behind our backs, we headed up the mountain to look for him. After much calling and shaking the nut bag, he came up to us and we slipped the halter on. Halfway down the

69

mountain he stopped dead in his tracks, sniffed the ground cautiously, and refused to move forward.

"Go on," we said, tugging on his halter. He reluctantly took one more step and his whole body, all fifteen hundred pounds of it, sank into a *sugre* (quicksand). He panicked, kicking wildly, his eyes bulging with fear. We were horrified. He couldn't get out, and he was sinking deeper. We tugged on his halter as he flailed with his front legs. Finally he got a purchase on solid ground, and with huge effort, hauled himself out. We had walked over that same ground, but he sensed that it would not hold him.

Day 4: We parked our wagon by the water at Killary Harbor, and put Scrooge to pasture. When we woke the next morning we saw that our wagon had sunk hubcap deep into the mud, and was really stuck. We got Scrooge and began to harness him when the farmer came running out of his cottage.

"You can't ask the pony to pull that out. You've got to do it yourselves."

There was something about the way he said it that made us suspicious. But we got some people from the other wagons to help and we all pushed and pulled until the wagon was up on dry ground. All the while the farmer was watching us with an impish grin, and Scrooge was whinnying and snorting because we were doing *his* job.

Day 5: Back at the estate we drove smartly through the gates knowing Scrooge would make it. We unhitched him for the last time and put him to pasture. He immediately fell on his side, rolling over and over.

"Oh, my God! We've killed him," we thought.

"He's in his health," said the stable hand, smiling.

We send Scrooge a Christmas card every year.

Scrooge in his health

CORRIDA

Nimes, France, May 1990

The Camargue is a huge delta area where the Rhone River flows into the Mediterranean Sea. It is full of birds, and it is home to herds of pure white horses with flowing manes. It is also home to the *ganadarias* (ranches) where fighting bulls are bred. They are herded by Guardians, the cowboys of the Camargue. They use long lances to herd them on horseback. The fighting bull must never see a man on foot until he enters the bullring in Nimes. This all sounds like it should be happening in Spain, but this is the south of France, very near Spain.

picador

In the nearby city of Nimes the bullring in the ancient Roman coliseum, built in AD 100, is empty. We are shown to the bull pens where we can see, through small windows, the bulls that will fight in today's corridas. They lie about, peacefully chewing their cuds, oblivious to their destinies. Nearby, the matadors go through their dressing ritual. Now we join the crowds that have begun to pour into the arena. Then the music begins, and the grand parade, or *quadrilla*, begins. First to enter the ring are the *alguaciles*, two horsemen dressed in seventeenth-century garb complete with plumed tricorns, who circle the ring in opposite directions at full gallop. When they pass each other the crowd roars. Next come the matadors in their dazzling suits of light, then the toreadors, and finally the picadors on horseback. Then come a team of horses with bloodred horse blankets and a row of tiny, colorful flags in their collars. Their drivers are dressed all in white with red berets and sashes around their waists. They are called *mulilleros*. Then the president of the corrida gives the *alguaciles* the key

SORTEO

Là

LA CORRIDA

Midi Libre

program

for the *toril*, the doors to the bull pens. They in turn give it to a man who will open the doors. Finally, all is quiet, and the doors to the bull pens are flung open. A fighting bull bursts into the ring, black as coal, with a huge chest and neck, and sharp, curved horns. The crowd gasps. A barb displaying the colors of his *ganadaria* has been jammed into the bull's neck muscles. The crowd cheers as the bull rampages around the ring, sometimes slamming into the barricades with his horns.

Now the toreadors step from behind the barriers and work the bull with their large pink-and-gold capes.

padded picador horse

The matador watches for dangerous traits in the bull's charge. Does he hook to the right or left?

Then the matador tries him out. Now it's the picador's turn. He rides out on his thinly padded horse and entices the bull to charge. The horse is blindfolded so he can't see the bull, but he sure can feel the thousand pounds of fury that slams into his flank. We've seen the horse and picador picked up on the bull's horns and thrown to the ground. The picador's job is to drive the lance into the bull's neck muscle and weaken it. The crowd boos if the picador works the lance too long. Finally the picador exits, and the banderilleros take over unless the matador does it himself. They run at the bull holding a colorful, barbed spear called a banderilla in each hand. As the bull charges, a banderillero leaps into the air directly over the bull's horns, and he drives the banderillas into the bull's neck. This is done three times. It is very dangerous, and the crowd loves it.

Now the bull is ready for the matador. The bull's head hangs low from its wounds. Blood streams down its flanks, the banderillas hanging from their barbs. The bull is enraged, and full of fight. The matador steps out from the barricade, and their ancient dance of death begins. It is very dangerous for the matador, but the bull *will* die at the end of the dance. The matador executes

faena

exquisite maneuvers as the bull charges. He works in closer and closer to the bull with each pass until his suit of lights is stained with its blood. The closer he gets, the louder the crowd roars, and the music will play if he is having a good *faena* (series of passes with the cape). He kneels before the bull, hands at his sides, enticing the bull to charge. It does. He's too slow getting up and the bull hooks him with his horns, tossing him in the air. The crowd gasps. He lands, rolls up onto his feet. His tight pants are ripped open by the bull's horns. The dance resumes.

The bull charges, head low. One horn drives into the sand, and it cartwheels onto its back. It struggles back to its feet and charges the matador again.

The corrida will only last twenty minutes because that's how long it takes the bull to figure out there's a man behind the cape, and how to gore him. That's when he becomes extremely dangerous. It is time to end the dance.

The matador asks the president for permission to kill the bull, then tosses his cap over his shoulder. If it lands right side up it's a good sign. If it lands upside down with its bloodred interior showing, it's a bad sign. If it lands that way, the matador will turn it right side up before beginning the final *faena*.

Now the matador faces the bull with a small cape called a *mulleta* inside of which is concealed a long, curved sword. The music stops. The crowd is hushed. They know what is about to happen. The matador maneuvers the bull until the bull is squared, the feet aligned so that the target is directly behind its horns. Then the matador leaps into the air, drives the sword between the shoulder blades, and spins off to the side, the bull's horns only inches from his heart. The bull stands mortally wounded, only the handle of the sword showing at his shoulder blades. The matador walks up to the dying animal and tenderly places his hand on the bull's forehead. The bull topples over. A *torero* runs

 in and, with a short dagger, gives the coup de grâce by severing the vertebrae just behind the head.

The crowd is ecstatic. The matador stands covered in blood in his jeweled suit of lights, and he acknowledges the crowd. He is awarded an ear for his clean kill and bravery. He and his *quadrilla* (entourage) parade around the arena with the severed ear in his hand. He stops, and tosses it to a special admirer. Some in the crowd throw objects into the ring to be touched, and thrown back by the matador, or sometimes as gifts, like flowers.

The *mulilleros* enter the ring, attach a chain around the bull's horns, and drag him out through the same door he entered the ring, leaving a trail of blood. If the bull was very brave he is applauded, and sometimes granted a *vuelta*, an encircling of the ring. The *toreros* leave each in turn with his *quadrilla* to great applause.

That corrida took place in the south of France close to Spain. Bull fighting is hugely popular in the south of France, even though the rest of France will deny it.

FERIA

Nimes, France, May 1990

It was the end of the week, and the last corrida was finished. By the light of the street lamps the two-thousand-year-old coliseum looked like an enormous hunk of crumbling blue cheese. Inside we were jammed in, not with ancient Romans, but with a crowd in blue jeans whirling tiny flashlights over their heads.

In searchlight circles in the center of the arena, trick riders galloped around a giant papier-mâché elephant. An enormous wooden effigy of a fighting bull was set afire, and the flames shot fifty feet into the night sky. The heat made an oven of the entire arena. We, along with twenty thousand other people, drew back.

Children in white tutus danced where bulls had died that very afternoon. Whirling dervishes of sparks on the sand illuminated the gore stains. A band played

Roman coliseum, Nimes

the song of Nimes and then the song of Provence. We all stood and sang reverently.

The mounted *alguaciles* who led the procession in the corrida were black cutouts

against the flames. Girls in bull costumes, horns on their heads, ran around the fire while fine boys in suits of light looking like they just stepped out of a Goya painting danced the polka. "The Beer Barrel Polka" was played on the accordion in the coliseum where Caesar once sat and turned his thumb down.

There were performers dressed like medieval rabble with red-painted faces. We watched as they ran from the arena like gladiators exhausted from their exertions in the heat of the flames into the catacombs below. They

flopped down on the
steps worn smooth by
the backsides of *real*
gladiators. One stuck
her tongue out at us,
looking like a gargoyle.

A girl on twelve-
foot-high stilts lurched
by in the stiff walk
peculiar to stilt walkers,
and disappeared into
the vomitorium where
Romans vomited after
gorging themselves.

The ceremonies inside the arena were ended in a blaze of fireworks and we, along
with the throngs, spilled out into the narrow streets full of smoke from the food tents.
Inside the tents were six-foot-wide pans of steaming paella. The streets were jammed
with people, camels, and Guardians, the mounted cowboys of the Camargue. Flamenco
dancers whirled and stamped their feet on makeshift stages.

The tiny underground bodegas were filled, stuffed like sausages, and still people
poured in to drink champagne and dance the Sevillana. Even the huge black bouncers
couldn't hold them back. Toreros made their appearances like rock stars to adoring fans.

In a street café a man in a fine suit sat eating "Gaurdian du Taureau," the meat of the
bulls killed that afternoon in the arena. The man daubed his mouth daintily with his
napkin and sipped a bit of rosé. A group of men in motorcycle jackets and wearing
earrings stood nearby. One of them had a pet black-and-white rat on his shoulder. This
revelry would go on all night.

NOVIADA

Nimes, France, May 1990

The bull had his back to the barricade. It was the one place in the ring where he felt safe. We were sitting in the first row and could have touched him. We looked over the bleeding hump of his shoulder with bright banderillas hanging from their terrible barbs, up the down-curved blade of the sword, and into the eyes of the young *novillero*. His suit of lights glinted and dazzled in the sun. He adjusted his position, raised up on one toe, and lunged over the horns. The sword made a soft, sliding sound as he drove it in up to the hilt. He spun off to the side, and the toreadors moved in. The bull swung his head from side to side at their tormenting capes. We could hear very clearly the grunts of their exertions, the moaning of the bull, and the slicing of gristle and flesh as the sword cut back and forth, back and forth with each swing of the head. Blood gushed from the bull's gaping mouth and lolling tongue.

permission to kill the bull.

The *novillero* stepped forward and waved off the toreadors. He placed his hand gently on the bull's head between the horns and waited. The bull uttered a deep, terrible bellow and fell to its knees, then toppled over, dead.

The slight young man in the dazzling blood-spattered suit turned, lifted his head, and raised his hand to the roaring crowd. He was now a full-fledged matador. He had killed his first big bull.

HARRY'S HARBOR BAZAAR

Frankfurt, Germany, June 1990

Up on a bluff in a dilapidated section of town facing the harbor was Harry's Harbor Bazaar. The favorite pastime of the people of Hamburg was to come here on a Sunday to browse. I don't think anyone ever bought anything.

Harry was less than five feet tall and had a long white beard and an old dog of indeterminate lineage. When you walked into the place it smelled like Harry's dog, or maybe like Harry. If they stood perfectly still you would think they were for sale along with all the other bizarre items that crowded every square inch of the floor, ceiling, and walls, and every narrow passageway in all the subterranean chambers that ran underneath the ground floor.

Harry

Harry's dog

There were masks from Bali, Venice, and Africa made of clay and feathers, and wood and china. Not a few, but dozens and dozens. There were old Arab fusils made of engraved silver and camel bone, battle-axes from New Zealand, dugout canoes from New Guinea, a whole room full of carved wood African fetish figures, all four feet high and standing at attention. It looked like pictures we'd seen of the excavated tomb of a Chinese emperor guarded by an army of hundreds of terra-cotta soldiers.

Another room was filled with Balinese shadow puppets, hundreds of them. In another, dozens of the same life-size gilded Buddhas all wearing the same beatific smile, Masai spears, Australian aboriginal spears and spear throwers. And boomerangs, carved wooden turtles, the shells of green sea turtles the size of which haven't been seen in years, a stuffed cocker spaniel and a little black dog. Racks of guitar-playing

shrunken head—.
extra charge

Elvises in painted ceramic along with dozens of Walt Disney's Goofy character done in the same medium. There were boxes and boxes of seashells from every ocean in the world: chambered nautilus, helmet shells, turbans, augers, and cones. There were hula girl ashtrays, carved coconut pirates, boxes of Barbie dolls, a stuffed lion, and a life-size carved wooden one. For a small charge, you could see shrunken heads.

Then there was this room, a kind of subterranean crypt, containing the stuffed remains of just about every creature in the world, a necrotic Noah's Ark. They were in boxes on shelves piled one on top of another all the way to the ceiling. There were a gray seal and a harbor seal, a wolverine and several other kinds of weasels, polar bears, baboons, and badgers. A red fox, boxes of ducks and seabirds, several horned grebes and great horned owls, penguins, pelicans, and porcupines. There were sacred ibis, and at least six great gray herons, one with its lower bill hanging limply, and only one glass eye. There were hedgehogs, several mute swans and a black swan, a moose head, and a tom turkey with its tail fanned out. There were several hooded cobras, a giant garial, and a serval cat missing its face. There were ring-tailed lemurs, monkeys, and meerkats. A leopard whose fur was rotting away, an otter, a scaled lizard, a decaying wolf, a Sarus

crane, and a black grouse all in unnatural, grotesque poses. There was a crumbling panda forever frozen in an odd posture with a lipstick-colored, wide-open mouth. On the floor with many other unrecognizable bits of skin and fur was the skin of yet another panda, dried leather holes where bright eyes had once been. There was an elephant foot wastebasket, and a stuffed chimpanzee holding a Masai spear.

Suddenly, we had to get out of there. We hurried down the narrow passageways past the beatific Buddhas, the hideous demon masks from Bali, past Harry's dog asleep next to the stuffed cocker spaniel, and past Harry himself who never spoke a word. Outside, happy to be among the living again, we took deep breaths of salt air as crying seagulls wheeled above us.

shadow puppets

THE HARD WAY

Kautokeino, Norway, 125 Miles above the Arctic Circle, April 1991

Betsy: "The trip would be much faster and easier by snowmobile," said our Sami guide, Ola.

"You don't understand," I said. "We want the experience of a reindeer sledge ride." Ola shrugged and walked toward a small herd of reindeer nearby. He moved slowly and cautiously into the group of half-wild animals, hiding a harness behind his back. Suddenly he lassoed a big stag, pulled him quickly in, and grabbed both antlers. Man and beast engaged in a desperate struggle, the reindeer tossing his antlers up and down, Ola, firmly gripping the antlers, flopping up and down like a rag doll. Ola finally brought the beast to its knees, deftly cinched him into a harness, then hitched him to a sledge. This seemed to calm the stag, and he stood, sides heaving from the battle, puffs of frost exploding from his nostrils.

This act was repeated with four more reindeer; two to pull our sledge, and two as spares to be tied behind our sledge. Ola then flopped several reindeer hides on the sledges for us to sit on, and took the lead. At last we were ready to go. Ola glanced over his shoulder at us. "Are you sure you want to do it this way?" he asked. "It would be easier by snowmobile."

"Yes," we assured him.

Ola told us it should be about a four-hour journey. The idea was to follow a frozen river across the Finnmark Plateau to Ola's winter camp where there was a much larger herd of reindeer. We would spend the night in a tepee called a *lavu*, experience a thirty-degree-below-zero night, and witness the awesome aurora borealis.

KAUTOKEINO IDRETTSLAG

REINKAPPKJØRING
i Kautokeino

Voksne   3008

KLEMET O HÆTTA Regnskaps- og veiledningskontor
Distr.repr. for UNI-forsikring

reindeer race ticket

Off we go!

Ola shouted a command to his reindeer, and it lunged forward. Our team lunged with a jerk that nearly threw Ted and me backward into the team behind us. That team had lunged forward, too, nearly tromping on our heads. Once a cadence was established the sledges ran smoothly over the packed snow. The soft, swishing sound of the blades, and the white world around us had a tranquilizing effect. But, soon I began to feel a warm wetness seeping up through my snow pants. Puzzled, I ran my mittened hand underneath my bottom. The mitten, once gray, was now red. Blood!? It didn't take long for me to figure out that the reindeer skins I was sitting on were not fully cured. Oh well, nothing to do about it. I started to relax again, leaning back on the sledge to enjoy the scenery. We had been traveling for about three hours now so according to Ola we should reach camp in another hour.

Just ahead of us was a low stand of birch trees in this world of unbroken white snow. It was a bit eerie gliding through the semidarkness of the forest, and a shiver ran up my spine. Suddenly, all the reindeer balked, snorted, then bolted through the birch forest as if being chased by demons. All hell broke loose. Ola struggled to control his animal, while the team

train wreck!!

82

Back on the trail

behind us leaped forward, one jumping over the sledge. Their ropes were now crisscrossed around my neck. The reindeer galloped forward while I made a desperate effort to tug the ropes away from my neck. Finally I ducked out from under them and rolled off the sledge into chest-deep snow, tipping the sledge over with me. Ted had jumped off the other side, and sat half-submerged in the snow, sputtering from a faceful of the white stuff. The scene was a tangle of ropes, antlers, flailing hooves, and Ola's barked commands as the reindeer struggled to sort themselves out. At length the exhausted animals lay still and panting, allowing Ola to step among them, unhitching and rehitching, freeing up antlers and hooves, and gently kicking the reindeer up to standing.

"Wolves," said Ola.

"Wolves?" we repeated.

"They remember when wolves were in these forests," he said as he trudged around picking up reindeer skins and supplies and loading them back on the sledges. It was way past four hours. Then he turned and, hands on his hips, looked back and forth between his two sorry-looking charges.

"I told you it would be easier by snowmobile," he said.

GYPSY HORSES

Ballinasloe, Ireland, October 1996

The horses came tumbling over the slippery stone steps like a black-and-white tidal wave. The sound of their metal-shod hooves clattered on the hard stone. The shouts of the Gypsies, and the sound of their whips were gut-wrenching. The steps were too steep for creatures this size all crowded together, unfamiliar. In their midst a lean, piebald trotting horse trapped in the shafts of a sulky tumbled headlong down with the tide, its driver whipping furiously. At the bottom of the stairs was a makeshift corral. Two days of rain and mud had now mixed with urine and manure. Gypsy boys, their faces streaked with dried snot, mud, and tears from their own whippings, whipped the giant horses across their rumps and feathered fetlocks. The horses whinnied and surged against the metal poles that had been crudely lashed together to contain them. The boys whipped them, and they kicked out with their hind feet. The Gypsy men stepped in with stout sticks and wielded them like batons in a riot. The horses tethered to the poles finally settled down. A redheaded Gypsy boy whipped them across their rumps, forcing them even tighter against the fence. He did this every few minutes. A passerby, annoyed by this cruelty, asked, "Why are you whipping those horses?" The boy looked up at him without expression, then whipped the horses again.

THE BATH

Ballinasloe, Ireland, October 1996

From a stone bridge we watched as the big piebald stallion with bright blue eyes stood shivering on the riverbank. The blond Gypsy had scrubbed him down with soap, and was now trying to pull him into the cold river Suck to rinse off the soap. The horse struggled, pulling against the halter. Another Gypsy stepped in and whipped it across the rump. The stallion fought valiantly and won as the blond Gypsy slipped and fell on the muddy bank. The halter was replaced by a hard bit. Then, more tugging and whipping. This time the stallion lost and went into the river. It was bitter cold. He whinnied and swam for all he was worth against the strong current, his piebald color blurred by the brown water. He gained the bank but, not yet free of the soap, he was whipped back into the river. The Gypsies finally let him climb back up onto the bank. Then they threw the foal in. The man standing next to us on the bridge said, "They know more about horses than anybody."

A few minutes later we heard the quick clip-clop of hooves on pavement, as the blond Gypsy galloped bareback on the piebald stallion. The stallion was brilliant white and black from its bath, and its long fetlocks were flying. That would bring more money at the fair.

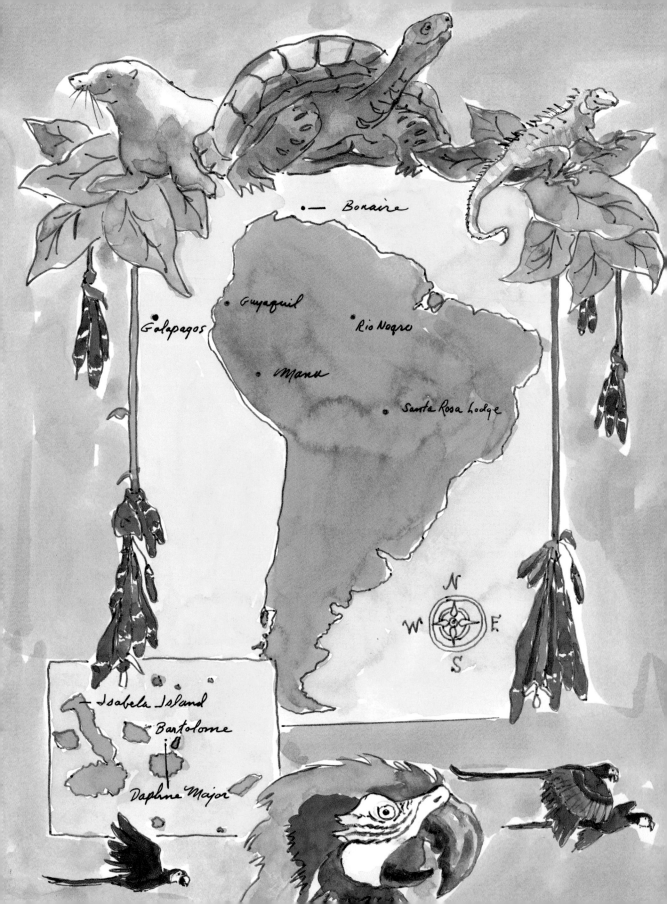

Bonaire

Galapagos

Guyaquil

Rio Negro

Manu

Santa Rosa Lodge

N
W · E
S

Isabela Island

Bartolome

Daphne Major

SOUTH AMERICA

TOWN PIER

Bonaire, Dutch Antilles, July 1984

Ted: I slipped on my scuba tank just as the tropical sun dove into the sea. I waded waist deep into the ocean alongside the town pier, bent over, pulled on my flippers, and adjusted my mask. The big oceangoing tugs that were moored at the end of the pier glowed with onboard lights, and as I sank below the surface, I could hear their generators humming. The water was crystal clear, and I could see the concrete pilings of the pier fading off into the eerie twilight gloom.

During the day the floor of the ocean under the pier looks like a litter-strewn dump, but now at night it blooms into a phantasmagoric flower garden.

I finned over to the ghostly pilings and turned on my light. They were covered from top to bottom with living things. Huge, orange-and-purple tube sponges reached out, and anemones of every size, shape, and color swept the water with their long, delicate fingers. Among them, arrow head crabs tinier than your little fingernail stuffed bits of food into their mouths with their claws.

I looked up and had an instant jolt of fear. The pilings reaching up to the surface and the reflections from my flashlight on the underside of the water made it appear as a solid ceiling. The sensation was that there was no way to break the surface. Like being trapped. I knew there was six feet of space between the surface of the water and the deck of the pier but, in the dark, the fear strikes every time. I looked down the row of pilings, wondrous life clinging to every square inch. I finned to the bottom twenty feet below. The discarded

On the bottom

tires and litter are home to moray eels gaping in breaths of water, and spotted drums with their high, elegant dorsal fins.

As I moved along the bottom, every old can or broken bottle held a living gem.

Now in thirty feet of water, I finned out from beneath the pier and over to the big tugboats moored there. I lay on my back on the sandy bottom just beneath the keel of a big tug. I reached up to touch the tons of tugboat floating just two feet above me. It seemed as if I was holding it aloft with my fingertips. I could feel the vibration of its generator.

I shut off my light and finned out into the open water. The bright night sky illuminated the bottom. I hung there suspended, weightless, and looked around me. I could see the massive bellies of the tugs, and the pilings made an ominous row of dark caves. Five shapes as large as me swooped in and wheeled off, then turned and headed toward me again. I switched on my light and into its beam swam five five-foot-long tarpon. Their broad sides covered with enormous scales glinted like silver dollars. Three times more they passed me, like creatures from the warm prehistoric seas.

THE ENGLISHMAN

Santa Rosa Lodge, Pantanal, Brazil, August 1988

We met an Englishman in the coastal rain forest of Brazil in a place called Itatiaia. He was a birder and had been traveling through Brazil for six weeks. He looked like he'd been down a dirt road or two. He kept a detailed journal in a bag he had slung over his shoulder. In tiny, careful script he listed every bird he had seen so far, common name, local name, Latin name, place, terrain, time of day, song, number of individuals, weather . . . everything.

We got to swapping bird stories, and we mentioned that we hoped to see the rare hyacinth macaw. He thumbed through his journal, ran his finger down a page, and there it was.

Arara, *Anodorhynchus hyacinthinus*, Santa Rosa in Pantanal, big tree near palm trees, 5:00 p.m., shrieking call, 9 birds, 85 degrees at sunset.

Two weeks later, and eighty-five bumpy miles on a dirt road in the Pantanal, a marsh the size of Pennsylvania, across one hundred rough log bridges, past millions of South American caimans laying piled on top of one another, anacondas longer than our combi, herds of ninety-pound rodents called

Vaqueiro

89

jucare

capybara, countless birds, and barefoot cowboys herding hump-backed cattle, we come to the end of the road, and the Santa Rosa Lodge on the Paraguay River.

At 5:00 p.m., just as the Englishman wrote in his journal, we heard shrieking calls, and set out in the tall grass heading for the big tree by the stand of palms right where he said the macaws would be. And there they were, just as the Englishman said. Suddenly, out of the tall grass came an enormous white Brahma bull with a huge hump on his back. Our hearts stopped. He eyed us up and down, pawed the ground, snorted, then crashed back into the tall grass. Why didn't the Englishman put *that* in his journal?

hyacinth macaw

BLUE AND YELLOW

Santa Rosa Lodge, Pantanal, Brazil, August 1988

Betsy: Besides the wild hyacinth macaws that can be seen there, the Santa Rosa Hotel has a pet blue-and-yellow macaw. It's very tame. It's fun to watch it crawl over the thatched roofs and hang by one foot, or use its hooked beak to crawl up the branches of trees.

One morning it was sitting on the handle of the water pump. We went over to talk to it.

"*Arara,*" said the macaw.

"*Arara,*" we answered. It was easier for us to speak its language than for it to speak ours. It flew up onto my shoulder. I was enchanted and touched that it had chosen me instead of Ted. Then it took my whole ear in its razor-sharp, bear trap of a beak, tasting it with its black tongue. I was no longer enchanted. I was *terrified*!

Ted laughed till he cried.

Don't hurt me!

RIO NEGRO

Brazil, August 1988

Ted: The sailor and the engineer have just returned from fishing. They have caught a big fruit-eating fish called a pacu, and a really big black piranha. They pull their skiff alongside our riverboat and tie up. The fish are flopping in the bottom of the skiff, gasping, slowly suffocating. They throw them up on deck. The black piranha's mouth is gaping open then snapping shut. It has razor-sharp teeth.

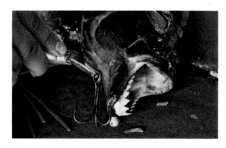

black piranha

The fishermen climb aboard and proceed to filet the pacu while it's still alive and flopping. I decide to put the piranha out of its misery, so I pick up a heavy stick from the deck and give the piranha a sharp blow behind its head. The blow is not sure, and the fish flops all the harder. The whole crew has gathered around and laughs heartily. My face reddens, but I'm determined to end the suffering of that poor fish. I hit it again as hard as I can. It flops even harder. They laugh even harder. I hit it once more with everything I've got. Finally, it lies still.

The crew speaks to one another in Portuguese. I ask my guide, Wilson, what they're saying. He says, "They say you enjoy killing."

fishing

92

THE PLAZA

Guayaquil, Ecuador, September 1991

In Guayaquil, just in front of the old cathedral, there's a beautiful plaza. It's called Plaza Sentinario or sometimes, more simply, Iguana Plaza. A statue of Simon Bolivar mounted on a rearing charger sits in the center of the plaza, and off to one side a cast-iron Victorian band shell painted dark green. On the other side is a large, half-filled pond. The whole plaza is enclosed by a tall, cast-iron fence with grand gates at either end. It is an island surrounded by heavily trafficked streets.

The great seal of Ecuador has been planted in flowers in the grass and is manicured daily. The plaza is ringed by palm trees and tall mahoganies whose buttressed trunks are painted white to a height of six feet. Certain of these trees are full of enormous iguanas. One doesn't see them at first. It takes a minute. Then they seem to be everywhere. They are green, gray, and the biggest ones are bright ocher. They bob their heads showing great throat flaps. They are draped over the topmost branches, resting in the forks or scraping down the trunks upside down.

little dinosaur

Someone brings lettuce for them, placing it around their favorite tree where they pile on top of one another to feed on it. Passersby stop and stare at them, bemused. Signs everywhere implore people to leave them alone.

In the heat-soaked evenings, the plaza is illuminated by very bright floodlights. Couples sit on the gracefully curved wooden benches and talk. Some kiss. A mad old woman stands up on the band shell talking incessantly about Jesus into a useless microphone. The iguanas are all up in the treetops sleeping. One is draped over a palm frond, swaying in the breeze, safe and secure. Somewhere in the trees with them is a three-toed sloth. Just one.

WILD HORSES

Cotopaxi National Park, Ecuador, September 1991

Towering above the high, barren plain rises Cotopaxi 19,500 feet of active volcano with a thirty-foot-thick cap of ice extending down its black cinder sides. It is a place of condors. A herd of wild Spanish barbs roams the plain below. The herd stallion is as black as a cinder, and lean as a jackrabbit.

We stop our vehicle and see how close we can get to the herd on foot. They are about one hundred yards away standing in a line, looking warily at us. We start toward them, walking one behind the other at a forty-five-degree angle to them. It will appear to them that we are walking sideways, when in fact we are shortening the distance between us. At about fifty yards they get nervous. A pregnant mare steps forward and stares at us intently. Suddenly, a young stallion runs out in front of the herd whinnying and snorting and shaking his head. He prances back and forth, mane and tail flowing, feeling his oats. We get even closer. At thirty yards we stop. The black stallion gathers the herd and leads them away up a sawtooth ridge.

Park permit
showing Cotopaxi

Later, up on Cotopaxi at fourteen thousand feet, the ice wall behind us, we look down on the plain almost a mile below, and we can see the whole kingdom of the black stallion.

GIANT TORTOISE

Isabela Island, Galápagos, September 1991

We just *found* it. It's as if it had always been there, waiting, as if the trees and vegetation grew up around it. It's a shock to come back after a while to find it had moved. It looked as big as a Volkswagon. Its shell looked like it was made of bronze hundreds of years ago, the bronze having been worn smooth by the touch of a thousand hands.

When we first approached, the tortoise drew its head in between its elephantine front legs, which seemed to force a long, snakelike hiss from deep inside. All that could be seen then was an enormous shell sitting abandoned on the landscape.

If you wait, the tortoise either feels the threat is gone or it gets curious. Its head slowly emerges from the bulwark of its huge, scaly legs and overhang of shell. It turns from side to side as it moves from deep shadow into light, and looks directly in your face. Its face wears a kindly, bemused expression. It has to be well over one hundred years old, as the plates on its shell are worn smooth. It was already out of the egg when President McKinley was assassinated. By the time the Wright brothers flew the world's first airplane, it was already big enough to have no natural enemies, save the whalers who took tortoises in great numbers for food.

What can the brief moments that we stand before it mean in its great, extended scheme of things? It's so old and still growing. How big can it get? When and how will it die? It doesn't look like it *can* die.

waiting for finches

THE STANDOFF

Bartolomé Island, Galápagos, September 1991

six feet away

On a very high dune overlooking Shark Bay she sat atop her nest, a huge pile of bone-white sticks, screaming a loud, high-pitched scream. In the bay below the manta rays drifted like black blankets just beneath the surface.

This Galápagos hawk was very beautiful, more owl-like than hawklike, especially from the front. She turned her head from side to side, then tipped it almost upside down, screaming all the while. We walked to within six feet of her. She was very tame, and we watched each other for a very long time. We left her, still screaming, sitting atop her stick throne, and went swimming with the white-tipped sharks.

Later, we spotted a different hawk hanging motionless in the sky above the dune, like a kite on a string.

Below him were the tracks of several female sea turtles that had climbed the dune to escape the overamorous advances of the males. Their tracks look like they were left by Sherman tanks.

The hawk slid off its position and drifted along the crest of the dune, rose up abruptly, and hung motionless as before. From a high black lava cliff came a piercing scream, the female hawk, backlit by the late sun. The airborne hawk swooped directly over her and hung there, the updraft rippling his golden sunlit wings. He slid off his hover and disappeared behind the dune.

We charged up the dune like buccaneers to see where he had gone. The sand was soft, and we reached the top gasping for air. Just over the crest, the hawk was sitting in the sand among the morning glories screaming at a large land iguana. Land iguanas are no longer found on this island. This must have been one of only three that we heard had been released here thirty years ago. No one had been able to find them since. The hawk just did. He screamed and looked to the sky for his mate, then back at the great black creature in the sand in front of him.

The iguana was much too big for him to kill. The hawk seemed to be looking for signs of weakness. The iguana stood its ground. We watched for a while, then left them there on the dune to work it out among the morning glories.

FLYING UNDERWATER

Pinnacle Rk.

permit

Bartolomé Island, Galápagos, September 1991

Ted: Just to the right of Pinnacle Rock the water gets very shallow and clear. The sun's rays dapple the light gray rocks below, and big hump-headed parrot fish nibble at the barnacles on the rocks.

A sea lion appears in front of me. She lifts her head out of the water, squints, shakes her head up and down, then ducks back in the water and looks at me from under the surface. Seals are doglike, but unlike dogs they have learned to fly underwater. They have muzzles like a dog, but their whiskers are very long and thick, and they can arrange them in ways that give their expressions a most human aspect. Their eyes, too, are different from dogs' eyes . . . almost demure. This one seems to bat her eyes at me as I lie on the surface with my mask and snorkel.

She swims right at me very fast, then veers off at a right angle without any overt action to cause it. She is showing off, I think. She makes a slow, sensuous circle underwater, letting tiny silver bubbles dribble from her mouth. She stops six feet from me and hangs at the surface, slowly sinks to the bottom, and very, very gently rubs her muzzle along the rocks, eyes half-closed. It's a very provocative display. She swims around me and drops out of sight behind a rock ledge. A moment later she floats back up, peeks over the ledge at me, bats her eyes, then turns and slips off into the slanting rays of the undersea sun.

98

THE CONSOLATION PRIZE

Daphne Major Island, Galápagos, September 1991

Ted: We were plowing through rough seas on our way to Isabela Island.

"I talked it over with Captain Fausto," said our guide, William. "He said Fernandina Island is too far. He said our boat is too small, and it would take too long. We'll never make it. We would have to sail all the way around Isabela Island into the open Pacific."

He saw the look of utter disappointment on our faces. We wanted to see the flightless cormorants on Fernandina, and now our hopes were dashed.

"We have a consolation prize, though," he

Betsy talking to masked boobies

said. "Because we are a small group we can take you to Daphne Major to see the masked boobies. Only a few scientists ever go there. There is only one small problem. There is no landing place."

We made a detour, and the next morning Daphne Major was on the horizon. As we climbed into an aluminum skiff called a *panga*, William said, "Do exactly what I tell you. When I say 'jump' jump! Don't hesitate, even for a second." He was so serious he made us uneasy.

As we approached the island, huge swells swept onto the black volcanic rocks carved into knife-edged ridges and whorls by the sea. We crowded into the bow of the boat with William. He said, "The rocks are razor sharp. Just do what I tell you, and you won't get hurt."

Our cook, Nilo, was in the stern of the *panga* manning the outboard. He gunned the motor, and we rode a huge swell up onto the rocks. He held the *panga* there with all the power it had. William jumped out onto the jagged rocks barefooted. We cringed.

Oh no! Not again!

The boat slid back off the rocks leaving William on a ledge six inches wide. We surged forward on the next swell. "Jump!" yelled William. Betsy leaped off into space, and the *panga* slid away again. I saw her

scrambling hand over hand up a razor-sharp perpendicular wall behind William. There was no place to stand next to him. Again the *panga* surged forward. My heart pounded. "Jump!" I jumped. I landed on the postage stamp–size ledge. "Climb!" he barked. I climbed up the wall like a spider. William climbed up behind me in his bare feet. The masked boobies were completely without fear of humans. We had to step over them as they sat on their eggs in the middle of the trail. On the rim of the volcano we looked down into its deep crater. It was filled completely with nesting boobies. They crowded on the slopes and the floor of the crater. We sat on the ground right next to them listening to their high-pitched whistling calls.

Our sojourn with the masked boobies was magical, tempered only by the knowledge that we had to get back into the *panga* the same way we got out.

JUNGLE WALK

Manu River Lodge, Peru, 2002

Here's what we learned on a night walk through the forest with our guide, Monika.

We saw in the beam of her flashlight an arachnid the size of a dinner plate called a scorpion spider. We learned that two of its eight legs are modified into six-inch-long antennae on either side of its head with which it feels its prey in the dark. Then it seizes its prey with scorpion-like claws, actually modified mouthparts.

Monika constantly shined her flashlight on the path in front of us.

"What are you looking for?" we asked.

"The fer-de-lance," she answered. "One drop of its venom can kill a man. It can bite twice in a second."

We walked close on her heels from then on.

By the light of our head lamps we saw a cicada that had just emerged from its shell and was drying its wings.

We learned that its shell has a place on the back that is like a little backpack where its wings were folded up in storage until that moment. We learned that it is the male cicada that makes the deafening buzz with its wings to attract females.

We learned that there are cockroaches as big as mice that look like living fossils.

We learned that bats sometimes nest in narrow slits in tree trunks where their young will wait patiently, upside down, for their dinners.

All of this we learned in a short walk on a narrow forest trail in a rain forest that stretches pristine and unbroken for hundreds of square miles. Imagine the things we didn't learn.

THE CLAY EATERS OF MANU

Manu River Lodge, Peru, 2002

We board the long dugout canoe in the pitch black, our flashlight beams casting flickering shadows. A heavy mist envelopes the forest along the river's edge. As we move downriver, tree shapes appear out of the mist, then fade. Soon we see the floating blind, a thatched hut with an outboard motor attached, moored in the middle of the river. We board and begin our wait. The sun comes up, a silver disc bathed in a soft pink glow. Soon the mist will burn off. We eagerly await the arrival of the flocks of red-and-green macaws, the clay eaters of Manu. The bank of the river where they will come to eat is called a "clay lick." It is rich in minerals that will help the birds neutralize the toxins in the fruit they eat. Ironically, the toxins are manufactured by the fruit to prevent it from being eaten.

The excitement begins as dozens of pairs of the birds fly in. At nearly three feet long, with gorgeous red-and-green plumage, they are one of the most spectacular birds on Earth. The trees bloom with color as the raucous birds begin to land.

The birds are nervous and timid. With their heads in holes in the bank, they will be exposed and vulnerable to predators. As they feel more secure, a few of them come to the lick to eat clay. This is the signal for our boatman to start moving the blind nearer to the bank, using a winch. Closer and closer we come, moving silently an inch at a time, finally stopping within seventy-five feet, directly in front of the lick. We lean forward and peer through the opening in the thatch, our hearts pounding.

Now here they come in a blaze of glory! More than one hundred strong they begin eating clay in earnest. The shrieking din never lets up. They are so full of personality. What characters! They hang upside

102

down on vines, stare at each other beak to beak, squabble and try to force one another out of the best holes. They eat chunks of clay held in their feet, bits of it dropping on the heads of the birds below. They cover the bank like a brilliant, feathered mantle. After a while, a few birds that have eaten their fill fly off to roost in the palm trees. They perch side by side and groom each other tenderly.

Suddenly, a lookout bird sounds an alarm. SQUAWK! The rest of the macaws explode from the lick in a gaudy, shrieking frenzy and are gone. High above, a harpy eagle circles.

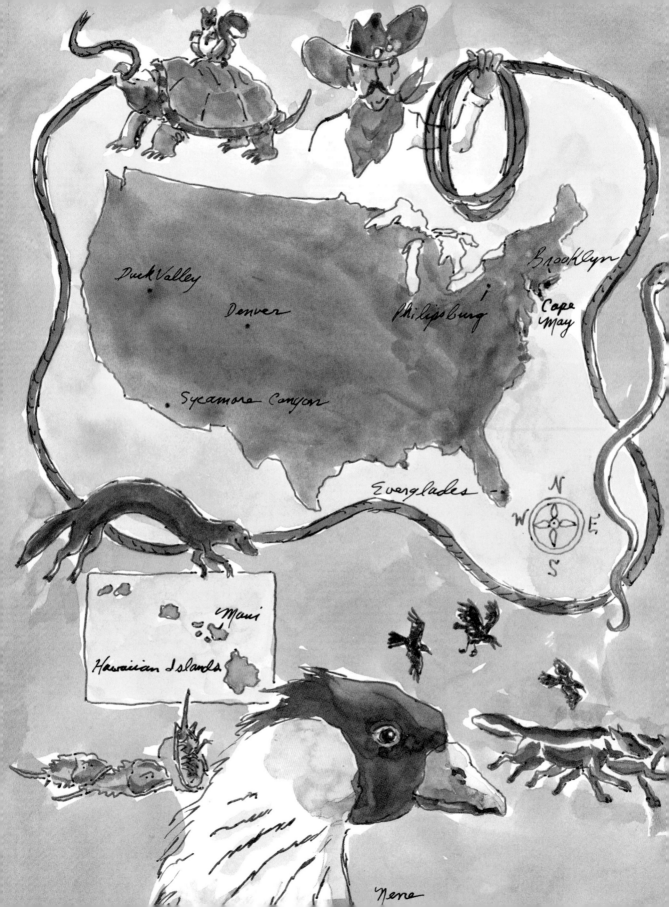

Duck Valley

Denver

Philipsburg

Brooklyn

Cape May

Sycamore Canyon

Everglades

N
W E
S

Maui

Hawaiian Islands

Nene

THE UNITED STATES OF AMERICA

THE CRATER

Maui, Hawaii, June 1973

We were staying with our friend King Curtis Iukea, a three-hundred-pound Hawaiian professional wrestler, in his A-frame house on the slopes of Haleakalā crater. Over a big bowl of "Portugee" (Portuguese) stew, he said, "Today we goin' into da cratah. You gonna see da nene!" With that, his eyes got as big as saucers.

We slipped on our backpacks while Curtis saddled his big palomino, Bobby Dee.

Attached to Bobby Dee's saddle was a saddle holster containing a Winchester rifle. "I'm gonna shoot us a goat," said Curtis confidently.

Goats are one of many introduced species that are decimating the native flora and fauna of the islands. They're fair game.

We dropped down over the lip of the crater, almost two miles high, and not far along the Sliding Sands Trail a big, black billy goat stood silhouetted majestically on a jagged lava flow. Curtis reined in Bobby Dee, slid his Winchester out of its holster, cocked it, raised it to his eye, and took careful aim. We held our breath. Time and the goat stood still. Curtis lowered the rifle. "Aww, I just can't shoot it," he said, shaking his head as he slid the Winchester back in its holster. We exhaled and moved on down the trail.

Walking across the crater floor three thousand feet down was like a walk on the moon. Jagged black rocks, hot on one side, cold on the other. We walked across huge lava flows, Bobby Dee carefully picking his way behind us. On the other side of the crater the whole scene changed. It was now lush and green due to the moisture spilling over

Curtis on Bobby Dee

the lip of the crater from the Kipahulu rain forest on the outside slope.

We climbed up to the Paliku cabin that was surrounded by forest and ferns called *paoli*, which Curtis gathered and cooked for us on the stove in the cabin. We were really tired after our trek. It was getting dark and cold. No one told us how cold it got

Silver sword

up there. We dumped our tent from its bag, looked at it, and realized we hadn't used it in a long time. We had completely forgotten how to set it up. The other campers were making bets that we would never get it up. It took us an hour, but we did it without once screaming at each other.

The next morning Curtis left us, and headed for the Halemauu Trail up and out of the crater. He cut quite a figure, three hundred pounds dressed all in black with a black, round-top ten-gallon hat, his long curly locks falling on his shoulders, sitting astride that big palomino. He turned and waved. We watched him till he was just a black dot in the distance.

That afternoon we hiked higher up the crater wall into a light mist. Then out of the mist came the fabled nene that Curtis had told us about. The Hawaiian goose flapped its huge wings, chest thrust forward, and honked loudly. It is one of the rarest birds in the world.

Nene

They were almost extinct in the wild, their numbers decimated by the introduction of rats and mongooses. They have been reintroduced on Maui by The Wild Fowl Trust, a captive breeding program in England. The nene has gorgeous white, brown, and black plumage with a rosy cheek patch that gives it a most beguiling expression.

A little farther up the trail we saw an even rarer sight, a silver sword. It's found only here above seven thousand feet. After twenty years it flowers but once, then dies. The next morning we wanted to watch the world-famous sunrise. We crawled out of our sleeping bags, faced east, and waited. There was a man sleeping next to us completely zipped up in his mummy bag. As the sun rose, the "mummy" sat bolt upright, unzipped his bag, snapped a picture, then fell back down. ZIP!

That day we packed up and headed for the Halemauu Trail, a terrifying, narrow switchback two thousand feet up the crater wall. Along the way we met men on horseback. The horses refused to walk on the outside edge of the trail so we had to back up as close to the edge as possible to let the horses pass.

Curtis with his dogs

Finally at the top, at ten thousand feet, we could see the entire crater floor below us and, on the other side, the sweeping Pacific and the curve of the horizon. We came to a very narrow land bridge with sheer drop-offs on both sides. Neither of us had the courage to walk across, so we crawled across on our hands and knees. When we stood up, there was Curtis with his big, smiling face.

"Let's go have a big bowl of Portugee stew."

THE CAPTAIN AND THE MONGOOSE

Maui, Hawaii, June 1973

After our two nights in the crater, Curtis took us to his father's ranch on the side of Haleakalā. There was much excitement around the barn when we arrived. "I caught me a mongoose!" said The Captain, Curtis's father, holding up a wire cage. The trapped mongoose paced frantically back and forth. Like goats, mongooses are imported and threaten the native wildlife.

"What are you going to do with him?" we asked.

"I'm gonna drown him," said The Captain. "He's not gonna steal my chickens." Then he marched purposefully to the horse trough, and plunged cage and mongoose into the water. Oddly, the cage was not locked. The door flew open when the cage hit the water, and the mongoose leaped through the air, hitting the ground running straight into the bush.

"Oh, well," The Captain said, smiling sheepishly. "I'll get him next time."

Somehow we knew he wasn't going to drown the mongoose any more than Curtis was going to shoot that goat.

I'm outta here!

TIT FOR TAT

Everglades, Florida, February 1974

Driving along the road in Everglades National Park we saw something odd in front of us and stopped. We looked through our binoculars at an astonishing scene. Five fish crows had harassed a red-shouldered hawk down onto the road. Two of the crows were holding the hapless hawk by his wing tips, pinning him to the ground. The other crows were pecking at him mercilessly, literally pecking him to death. Held down like that, the hawk was unable to bring his fierce talons into play to defend himself. It was awful. We couldn't watch any longer. We opened the car door and stepped out. The crows reluctantly

Looking for dinner

let go of the hawk and flew off. The hawk sat on the road, wings spread limply, still dazed by the beating. Finally he roused himself and took off. Later in the day he would probably snatch a baby fish crow in his talons, pluck it with his hooked beak, and swallow it whole.

Dinner!

PRETTY LITTLE THING

Everglades, Florida, February 1974

Betsy: The Bear Lake Trail in the Florida Everglades had suddenly changed from wide-open water and grasses to a dense green tunnel through the mangroves. It was nearly impossible to use our paddles, so we started pulling the canoe along by grabbing the overhead branches of the mangroves.

I was in the front of the canoe, and reaching up to grab a branch, I saw right next to my hand a pretty little black snake draped over a branch just above my head. I had almost touched it. Sleek as patent leather, with a gleaming shoe-button eye, it lay motionless, undisturbed by our arrival. We turned the canoe at an angle so we could both get a good view of it. We stuck our paddles straight down into the water to steady the canoe so we could lean even closer. We now noticed its snowy white throat. Inches away from it, I peered into its eye.

"It doesn't look dangerous," I said, remembering that poisonous snakes are supposed to have vertical pupils. This snake's pupils appeared to be round.

We stayed awhile, almost mesmerized by those shiny little eyes. Then we ducked as low as we could underneath the snake, pulling the branches on either side of the canoe to ease us forward, leaving the snake to its peaceful snooze.

Farther along the trail we met a park ranger in his canoe. We described the snake to him.

"Oh, that's your cottonmouth," he said. "Good thing you didn't get bit. First your blood turns to water, then your flesh starts to rot, then you'll wish you were dead."

BROADWING KETTLE

Cape May, New Jersey, October 1982

A hundred or more broad-winged hawks all swirling in a madcap maelstrom, others rushing across the sky on spread wings to join their fellows, plunge into the counterclockwise swirl. None go against the grain. They are like dry leaves caught in a dust devil. The momentum, like centrifugal force, quickens and they spin and rise thousands of feet into the sky and are spewed out the top. They slide off on spread wings and tails, lose altitude, and look for the next free ride up.

STORM FRONT

Brigantine, New Jersey, October 1984

We were standing on one of the dozens of dikes that crisscross Brigantine National Wildlife Refuge. A gyrfalcon had just flown over a pond of ducks putting them up in a panic.

Arching the salt marsh was a vast expanse of sky. The horizon was a brilliant white slash below black storm clouds that rose thousands of feet into the sky. We looked through our binoculars. In front of those clouds was a mass of birds so dense it looked like a swarm of locusts. They were coming at us, being pushed by the storm front at great speed. During their migrations, birds love a day like this to get a free ride.

The swarm was upon us now, directly overhead. We craned our necks, and through our binoculars saw thousands of snow geese, Canada geese, and many kinds of ducks, mallards, pintails, gadwalls, and shovelers among them. They weren't flapping their wings. They just let the storm front do the work. And the *sound*!! We could distinctly hear all their honking and quacking, like a giant celebration in the sky. The swarm zoomed past us in an instant followed by ominous, black storm clouds.

ROADHOUSE

Philipsburg, Pennsylvania, September 1985

Ted: The roadhouse was deserted and out of business like the nearby town. The town had been a mill town, bustling, a nice little town in its day. Now the main street was deserted or for rent except for Dick's Kitchen where the old-timers went for breakfast and company.

Big as a washtub!

The roadhouse sat on the edge of a tiny marsh. Its blacktop parking lot built on landfill pushed out into the marsh. The marsh was hemmed in on all sides by roads. It was early morning, and the marsh looked as deserted as the town and the roadhouse.

I sat in the parking lot on a big log barrier put there to stop customers from backing their cars into the marsh . . . when the roadhouse had customers. The sun was just peeking through the trees, and the gray mist that clung like gauze to the cattails began to burn off. An enormous snapping turtle hauled himself out of the ooze and came onto the road. He was as big as a washtub and covered with algae. He crossed the road and disappeared into a drainage ditch.

Then the birdsong began. First the redwing blackbirds appeared at both ends of the marsh. Clinging to the cattails one sang, "This is my territory," and "This is mine," sang the other. They backed up their claims by flashing their brilliant red epaulets.

As the sun struck the top branches of a willow tree, a king bird sat bolt upright, surveying his realm. He flew off, hawked an insect, then went back to his perch. Song sparrows began their sweet, warbling melodies, showy black spots called stickpins in their puffed-up breasts. Looking like a falcon with its swept back and pointed wings, a mourning dove landed on a telephone wire, adding its mournful note to the chorus of birdsong. Two black ducks flew in, curved their wings, and slipped into the water at the far end of the marsh.

I saw movement in the drainage ditch just below the parking lot embankment. "The snapping turtle's back and after the ducks," I thought. It wasn't the snapping turtle, but a muskrat. He swam down the ditch like a little beaver, slid up on the muddy bank, rooted around, then slipped back into the water directly below us, finally swimming through a culvert under the road.

I hadn't noticed until then that stacked by the culvert were long sections of large plastic pipes.

They were piled below the verge and on the other side of the road. We wondered what they were for. Surely not to drain this marsh, for if they did, then it, too, would be deserted and out of business just like the roadhouse and the town.

Looks like a little beaver

HOMER PIGEON

Brooklyn, New York, 1985

We found him squealing on our front stoop. "Pretty little pigeon," we thought. Then we noticed it had bands on its legs. "It must belong to someone," we thought, "a young homing pigeon."

It didn't seem to be able to fly, and it allowed us to pick it up. We called a friend who kept exotic pigeons. "Take it to the Meeker Pigeon Exchange," he said.

The Meeker Pigeon Exchange was a storefront in Brooklyn crammed full of cages crammed full of pigeons. We opened our pigeon's cardboard box, and the pigeon man said, "Oh, it's a squealer. That's what we call the young ones." He lifted it out of the box, expertly holding its legs between his fingers and cradling it in his hand. He studied the leg bands. "It's from Long Island. Flew maybe sixty miles, then got lost."

"Can it fly?" we asked.

"Let's see."

The pigeon man grasped the tip of its tail between his thumb and forefinger, and let go his other hand. The pigeon flapped both wings furiously, flying for all he was worth, his tail held tightly in the pigeon man's grasp. For the next two minutes, the three of us stood there as the pigeon flapped in place, heading for Long Island.

"He can fly," said the pigeon man.

THIRST

Sycamore Canyon, Arizona, May 1988

Betsy: "NO TRESPASSING OR WE'LL BLOW YOUR HEAD OFF" read the sign on a fence near the entrance to the canyon trail. We hurried past it, and on to the trailhead.

There we found a stand that held an empty registration book, and a dried-out ballpoint pen dangling from a string. We looked at each other and laughed. No one knew where we were so it made no sense to register anyway.

"Be sure to carry plenty of water, and it wouldn't hurt to have your desert survival book with you. The desert is unforgiving." This was the advice of a friend who had hiked the trail. He also told us to look for the five-striped sparrow, a bird found mainly in Mexico, but that could be seen in southern Arizona, too.

Our plan was to hike until we had drunk half our water then turn around, and head back. The morning was cool and bright as we scampered down the trail at a good clip sighting Mexican cardinals and hooded orioles along the way, but no five-striped sparrow yet.

The sun was getting hotter the deeper we descended, and we soon realized that we had drunk a bit more than half our water supply. Reluctantly we turned and headed back up the trail. Funny, we hadn't noticed how steep the trail was on the way down. The sun was high now, and the canyon was a furnace. Sweat rolled from under our hats and down our scarlet faces. Our shirts were soaked, and our pant legs stuck to our knees as we labored upward. We had drunk the last drops of water now, and we were starting to get really thirsty.

Suddenly, we were faced with a series of huge boulders that seemed to step up all the way to the sky. Funny, we hadn't noticed those on the way down, either. "Where did these come from? I don't remember climbing down them," I said. "Me neither," said Ted. Our tongues were beginning to swell from thirst, and we were beginning to get delirious. I squinted up at the sun. Our water was gone, and we were exhausted. The heat was taking its toll on our ability to think straight. No one knew we were there. We hadn't passed another soul. We didn't have the strength to search for the trail. All I could see were the newspaper headlines: "Two hikers' bodies found off the trail in Sycamore Canyon." "Two dumb hikers," I thought.

As we struggled up over the boulders our throats were so dry we could hardly talk, and we were beginning to panic. When we dragged ourselves over the top boulder we realized we were in a box canyon with no way out. Now we were really panicked. The canyon that was so beautiful in the morning had become a furnace bent on killing us.

The compass! Suddenly I remembered that we had a compass, and told Ted to look at it. "What good will that do," he said. "We don't know what direction to take." But, he got it out anyway and looked at it. When we looked at the compass we realized we were going west. With our last shred of reasoning power we realized that the right trail had led south toward Mexico. Now we should be going north! We had unwittingly strayed onto a side trail that led us up, into this box canyon. We had no choice but to retrace our steps until we found the trail. We could barely think or talk, much less climb down the huge boulders with shaky legs and our heads spinning. When we finally reached the last place that looked familiar to us we checked the compass again, and looked north. There was the right trail in front of us as plain as could be. We were so close to the trailhead we could see the sun glinting on our car. I croaked out a "Hallelujah!" and we stumbled up the last few, steep steps to the top. In the car were several gallons of water, and our desert survival book right where we left them.

We never did sight the five-striped sparrow.

SQUIRREL

Brooklyn, New York, April 1990

The tree men came and chopped up his home. They took half the tree away—half his home. They weren't good tree men. They didn't even have a chain saw to do the job right. They used machetes. When they were through there were raw wounds and splintered stubs of branches everywhere on the tree.

We saw the squirrel come back at twilight and venture down a main branch that had been spared. He crawled down it very slowly. It was now all unfamiliar. He held on tightly with the claws on his hind feet and smelled everything thoroughly. "Where was this branch? Where was that branch, the one that took me to the next tree? I can't get there this way. I'll try up here."

He sniffed the splintered end of a severed limb. It was gone. He leaped to the only main branch left, climbed it, and crawled gingerly out onto a tiny branch that had escaped the tree men's machetes. The thin branch sagged under the squirrel's slight weight, and he scampered back to the main trunk. A pair of mocking birds flew in chacking to each other. They seemed lost and flew on. It was their tree, too.

The squirrel stayed for a long while hanging by his hind feet, his tail flicking. He put the whole new scheme of things into his computer. He'd make do. He scampered up the old familiar main branch and flung himself into the next tree. He knew that one by heart.

PYRAMID LAKE

Nevada, June 1992

Pyramid Rock

When people speak of the lake they speak in reverent voices. It's a sacred lake, sacred to the Numa or Paiute people, the eaters of the cui-ui fish that live in the lake. Its natural stone pyramid is made of creatures of ancient seas. It is larger than the pyramids of Egypt, and it shines golden in the morning sun. Nearby there is a rock in the shape of a weeping woman called "the stone mother." It is her tears for her lost children, say the Numa, that created the lake. It is a place of bubbling geysers and hot springs.

It was a calm, sapphire noon lake, then an angry gray evening lake whose frigid, roaring winds threw fine sand into our eyes. They drove us into the back of our station wagon and into our sleeping bags.

At first light, propped up in our sleeping bags, we looked out through the rectangle of the station wagon rear door window. Geyser steam danced in the air. The vehicle vibrated and pulsed as the scalding geyser blew skyward with the earth's original heat.

Scalding hot!

ROUNDUP

Duck Valley, Nevada, June 1992

He sat, a hulk of a man, in a wheelchair in front of the cattle chute. A flock of yellow-headed blackbirds wheeled in the air and landed near him. We walked up to him, shook his hand, and, looking at the birds, told him we'd never seen them before. He looked over his shoulder at them, then back at us, and said, "You mean the ones with the yellow tops?"

The big man in the chair was Emmett, a Shoshone/Paiute buckaroo who had lost the use of his legs in an auto accident. A blue heeler with one bad eye and a hind leg that dangled uselessly ran up beside him. "His name is Lucky," said Emmett.

Emmett had to trade his horse for a specially equipped pickup truck. He was going to take us to watch their cattle roundup. All the buckaroos from the Duck Valley Reservation were taking part. They had come from all over, Indian rodeo buckaroos, friends, and neighbors.

The next day at first light, all the buckaroos mounted and headed for the mountains. We joined Emmett in the pickup and followed a rough dirt track. We came to a gully with a barbed-wire fence with a closed gate across it, and high hills all around. "I'll pick you up later," said Emmett as he dropped us off by the fence.

Silhouetted against the sky were several thousand head of cattle. Buckaroos moved in and out of the mass with whirling lariats over their heads. We could just make out

shouts and whistles, and the moaning and lowing of cattle. Mothers and calves were cut from the main herd by buckaroos on horseback and blue heelers. The dogs instinctively herded the strays and brought them around to the whistles of the men. Small groups of men, with their cattle already cut from the herd, waited. They stood like mounted brigades waiting for the call to battle. More and more small groups formed up and waited in the dust. Some of the riders were women and kids, every bit as good as the men.

The gate at the foot of the gully opened, and the first group moved out. The small herd was ringed tightly by a dozen buckaroos. They turned and headed up the hill toward us. We got as close to the fence as we could. A calf broke loose and ran toward us with a buckaroo in hot pursuit. They passed within three feet of us at a full gallop. We could hear the slap of leather, the tense voice of the man urging the horse on, and its snorting exertions. The ground shook beneath our feet as they raced by. A moment later the entire herd moved by, the buckaroos whistling and twirling lariats and leather quirts over their heads. They were so close they pressed us into the barbed-wire fence. Finally they passed us and disappeared around the bend.

Out of the dust Emmett appeared in the pickup. "Hop in the back. You'll get a better view." We headed down into the valley and pulled up alongside

121

"Heeler"

Emmett's herd. They had spread out some and were being moved at a leisurely pace, the buckaroos jaunty and relaxed in their saddles, the dogs nipping at the heels of the cattle. An hour later we crossed a high meadow and the cattle were herded tightly into a temporary metal corral.

Nearby sat a gas broiler with red-hot branding irons thrust into it like banderillas, the long barbs used by matadors. A calf was cut from the herd by the buckaroos using head-to-heel roping. Its mother cried piteously. The calf was held motionless on the ground by the horses that kept tension on the ropes. A team of buckaroos moved in. They knelt on the calf and branded it with a red-hot iron that sizzled and smoked. Another buckaroo cut a notch in one of the calf's ears, and a third castrated it with a razor-sharp pocket knife. This was all over in ten seconds. The calf was then released to its mother, and wandered off with her, a little dazed, but no worse for the wear.

122

AMPHIBIOUS LANDING

Cape May, New Jersey, May 1998

The landing

In May on Delaware Bay when the moon is full and the tide is high, they come ashore by the millions, like an armored amphibious landing, a landing that's been going on for three hundred and fifty million years. These are the horseshoe crabs coming ashore to lay their eggs, the eggs that will sustain a million shore birds on their long migration from South America to the Arctic Circle.

Long before birds came into being, horseshoe crabs began laying their eggs on land to protect them from predators in the sea. As we walk along the beach, the shore is a thick scum of milky green eggs rolling with the surf. The big female crabs come ashore with the smaller males grasping their shells with special hooked claws. Sometimes several males will hook together behind a female. She will deposit her eggs seven or eight inches down in the sand and the male will pass over the nest to fertilize them. In the crush the next crabs will rile up the nest, and the eggs will get pushed to the surface where the birds will gorge on them.

One species of bird gorging on these eggs is the red knot. These birds have come four thousand miles nonstop from South America and they are starving. One bird can

laughing gulls feasting

eat nine thousand eggs a day, and will double its weight in two weeks' time. If they have to linger here too long to feed it will cut into their short nesting season in the Arctic, and if they don't gain enough weight they won't be strong enough to lay a full clutch of eggs. And without the horseshoe crab eggs they wouldn't make it at all.

We meet a researcher collecting some crabs along the shore. She takes a sample of their blood and releases them. The blood is for use for medical research. She shows us a vial of the blood. It is bright blue.

The beach is awash now with lines of crabs hooked together and piled on top of one another. Some are on their backs with their spikelike tails stabbing the air. We resist the desire to right them, allowing nature to take its course. The birds, laughing gulls, ruddy turnstones, red knots, and sanderlings, feed furiously in among the crabs. Flocks of gulls screech above looking for a place to land and join the feast. This goes on for miles and miles of beach.

At the end of the day the beach is strewn with broken or overturned shells of these living fossils, like pictures we've seen of World War II amphibious landings on Guadalcanal or Iwo Jima.

end of the road

THE PIGEON

Brooklyn, New York, 1999

We think about him a lot, the pigeon in the subway station. He's trapped two levels below the street. He's been down there for a year. We see him every time we take the A train. He never sees the sky, the platform ceiling being his permanent hard, gray sky. We wonder what he eats, walking pigeon-toed along the cement floor of the station. Waiting for our train we see him burst into the stifling air, graceful and strong, with nowhere to fly.

Outside his brothers fly the city streets in flocks. There are the "street rats" surviving on handouts of day-old bread, and there are the coop pigeons that live in coops on city rooftops, the homers, the flights, and the tumblers who fall as if wounded only to soar up again into the sun.

Pigeons left their cliff homes in Africa eons ago to follow humans and to live in the structures they built.

They spread all over the world. This one is a New York City pigeon. He's lost. He wants the sky, but can't find it. While we wait for our train, we think about catching him and giving him back the sky, but we can't get near him.

Once, down here on the subway platform, we plucked a butterfly from the hair of a lady who was terrified of it, and put it back outside on a flower.

Brooklyn, New York, September 2000

"KENNEDY AIRPORT, $30—PENN STATION, $25—ANYWHERE IN THE BRONX, $30"

The price to get almost anywhere in the city was posted all over the front window. Inside was one big room with a map of the city and exotic travel posters all over the walls. We wondered what it would cost to hire a car to Tahiti. A driver slouched in one of the broken-down chairs pushed up against the wall. A bulletproof plastic partition separated the front and back rooms. There was a small trapdoor in the partition to safely hand money back and forth, but the door between the rooms was wide open.

Behind the partition was a fat man the size of a hippo. The office chair he was sitting in disappeared beneath rolls of fat as did the phone receiver he held between his ear and his shoulder. He scribbled addresses on a pad with fingers the size of bananas. He looked up at us, each of his many chins covered in stubble, and said, "I'll be right witchooze." It was then we noticed it.

Behind him, all along one wall, was a fish tank set on a tabletop at eye level. It was eight feet long with about ten inches of water in it. It was the movement that caught our attention. In the tank was a five-foot-long South American caiman. In the wild they are very shy and slide into the water if you approach them. This one moved toward us at our approach, and pressed the side of his toothy, grinning face against the glass with an unblinking, yellow dinosaur eye, a kaleidoscope of glints and specks of gold and black. Frighteningly vital and rapacious, it moved even closer, still grinning, its tail swishing back and forth, hungry, waiting.

"Mice," the fat man said, anticipating our question. "He drowns them first. Where to?"

NATURAL HISTORY

Denver, Colorado, October 2003

Ted: I was in the Museum of Nature & Science. I had just finished a talk on my latest book *Lost City: The Discovery of Machu Picchu*. The director of events came up to thank me and said, "Come to my office and I'll give you some passes for IMAX."

I followed her through the Hall of Natural History. There was an exhibit with stuffed, blue-footed boobies dancing like the ones I saw on Hood Island in the Galápagos. Also a stuffed giant tortoise just like the one I saw grazing in the mist one morning on Alcedo volcano. I wanted to tell her this, but didn't.

We passed another exhibit. This one showed a magnificent pair of gemsbok standing in tall *Aristida* grass. I'd seen a pair just like them in the Kalahari and got to within fifty feet of them as I crept through the tall grass. I didn't tell her this, either. I looked around. There wasn't a living soul in the hall. No one looking at these natural wonders that were conjuring such memories for me.

We passed a seabird exhibit with stuffed puffins and kittiwakes. It looked just like the cliffs in the Pribilof Islands that I'd hung precariously over to get my photos. I kept this to myself as well.

Finally, we left the deserted hall and stepped into the real world. A mile-long line of people snaked through the building waiting to see the IMAX film *The Coral Reef*, just like the one I dove on Heron Island, Australia.

We passed the new planetarium where you could see the sky projected onto the ceiling like the sky I'd seen in Lapland one night at forty below zero, but without the aurora borealis, I'm sure. There were huge crowds of kids and their parents doing all manner of things on interactive video screens. The screens flashed and flickered and beeped and booped. The kids loved it.

I followed the director down a flight of stairs into the bowels of the building. The narrow hall to her office was lined with rejects from the Hall of Natural History that were being phased out. There was a huge stuffed wolf, bigger than the white wolf I'd seen spook a herd of bison in the Northwest Territories, a smallish polar bear, half

the size of the 1,800-pounder I'd seen dozing on the beach in Churchill, and a snarling leopard just like the one I'd seen up a tree one night in the Okavango gnawing on an impala skull. A man pushing a clothes rack on wheels came out of a side room. We stopped to let him pass. The clothes rack was hung with dozens of spotted, striped, and furry animal skins.

I looked through a window into a classroom. It was darkened except for a light on the speaker. The backs of the audience's heads were in silhouette. The speaker held up a large crocodile skull and pointed to its snout. At the end of the hall by the director's office was a huge bull Pribilof fur seal, like I'd seen when the fog finally burned off on St. George's Island revealing a herd of two hundred thousand seals. Someone had left a pair of work gloves on its head.

The director gave me the passes and told me to enjoy the show. I went upstairs, hurried past the line still waiting for showtime, and emerged into the sunshine . . . where a pack of life-size, bronze wolves loped along among the real rocks.

PALE MALE

New York, New York, August 2007

We got off the bus one day at Sixty-Third Street and Fifth Avenue. Above the sound of the traffic we heard the unmistakable cry of a red-tailed hawk. No one around us noticed. We looked to the sound and just above us in a maple tree at the edge of Central Park was a red-tailed hawk. "It's got to be Pale Male," we thought. "The one that nests on the big apartment building by the park." A pigeon was dangling from his talons, flapping and struggling for its life. No one around us even looked up. Suddenly, a dozen or more crows, cawing loudly, swooped in and began to harass the hawk. They dove at him and he ducked each time. The poor pigeon flapped even harder.

Pale Male gave a high-pitched cry and there came an answering cry. Moments later, coming in like a fighter plane on a strafing run, came Lola, the female. She scattered the crows in one pass and wheeled off through the trees. Pale Male launched himself and his catch out of the tree, screaming all the while, flew fifty feet, and landed atop a dead tree trunk. Suddenly the tree became a totem pole topped by a mythical winged creature. Pale Male bent over the struggling pigeon and neatly killed it with his hooked beak. Then he began to pluck its feathers.

Now, people began to notice. A schoolteacher walking by pointed it out to her class. A businessman with a briefcase stood there openmouthed. A maintenance man from the apartment building across the street ran up and called someone on his cell phone. "You're not gonna believe what I'm lookin' at right now. It's like the wilderness."

Red-Tailed Hawk – Lewis 1998

AND ONE MORE . . .

MERCY FLIGHT

Manu, Peru, September 2002

late plane landing

Ted: Our ten days at Manu were over. We were standing on the jungle airstrip swatting mosquitos, waiting for our plane, which was very late. We asked our guide, Monika, "Why is the plane so late?"

"They're always late," she answered. "But not this late."

We waited. And waited. Finally we heard the drone of an airplane, and the little Cessna Caravan came over the treetops, landed, and taxied back to where we stood. The plane's prop was a spinning blur, and the noise from its big Pratt and Whitney engine was deafening. The pilot opened his window and motioned us to hurry. We picked up our duffels, and ran around the back of the plane. The side door swung open, and three steps folded down. The copilot yelled, "Hurry! Get in!" We ducked inside the plane. It was almost full. The pilot urged us to sit quickly.

It was then we noticed a hanging IV, and a little Indian girl spread across two seats, her head resting in her father's lap. One arm and one leg were bandaged. We stepped carefully over her injured leg and sat in the seats in front of them. Monika sat across the narrow aisle, and let the girl rest her leg in her lap. The copilot slammed the back door, locked it, and moved, half bent over in that cramped interior, to

130

the cockpit. The plane immediately taxied to the end of the field and roared into the air, barely clearing the trees, then flew out over the Madre de Dios River as it gained altitude.

The little girl was about seven years old, and her big black eyes were full of pain. Her father looked distressed. Monika spoke to the father in Spanish, asking him what happened. "He says his daughter was bringing his lunch to the gold mine in the jungle where he works when a big wind broke off a tree limb that fell on her, breaking her arm and leg. This plane made a detour to pick her up and get her to the hospital in Cuzco."

We felt so sorry for her. Betsy asked Monika to find out what was her favorite animal. "Monkey," said the little girl. Betsy got out her sketchbook and drew a silly monkey, passing it over the seat to her. She looked at it a long time, but didn't smile. Betsy drew another, and another, one funnier than the last. Each time those huge black eyes took them in, but still no smile.

The plane touched down in Cuzco thirty minutes later. The back door flew open. Two men unfastened the little girl's seat from the floor of the plane and gently lifted her out, seat and all. As they rushed her away we saw that she was still clutching Betsy's drawings tightly in her hand.

CONTENTS

Numbers in **bold** indicate pages with illustrations

A

Africa, first trip to, 5, 7–10
Antelope, 11, **11**, 19
Arizona, Sycamore Canyon hike, **104**, 116–117, **117**
Aurora borealis, 1, 127
Australia and Heron Island, 3, **42**, 51–52, **51**, **52**, 127

B

Baboons, 10, **10**, 34
Baikel, Lake, Mongolia, **42**, 61–63
Ballinasloe, Ireland, and Gypsy horses, **66**, 84–85, **84**, **85**
Bartolomé Island, Galápagos, **86**, 96–98, **97**, **98**, **99**
Berber rugs, 22, 24
Bison (buffalo), 1, 127
Bonaire town pier, Dutch Antilles, **86**, 87–88, **87**, **88**
Botswana: Kalahari, 4, **6**, 12–19, 127; Okavango Delta, Xakanaxa Camp, 6, 33–41, **33**, 128
Brazil: Iguazu Falls, 3; macaws in, 90–91, **90**, **91**; Rio Negro, **86**, 92, **92**; Santa Rosa Lodge, **86**, 89–91
Brigantine National Wildlife Refuge, New Jersey, 112, **112**
Brooklyn, New York: car service caiman, 126, **126**; location of, **104**; pigeons, 115, **115**, 125, **125**; squirrels, 118, **118**
Bull fighting, 71–77, **71**, **72**, **73**, **74**, **75**, **76**

C

Cape hunting dogs, 1, **1**, 19
Cape May, New Jersey, **104**, 111, **111**, 123–124, **123**, **124**
Chimpanzees, 4, 29
Chitwain National Park, Nepal, 2, **42**, 43–46, **44**, **45**, **46**
Colorado, Denver natural history museum, **104**, 127–128, **128**
Cotopaxi National Park, Ecuador, 94, **94**
Crater Lake Hotel, 29, 31
Crocodiles, 2

D

Dalanzadgad, Mongolia, **42**, 64–65
Daphne Major Island, Galápagos, **86**, 99–100, **99**, **100**
Denver, Colorado, natural history museum, **104**, 127–128, **128**
Donkey saddlebag, 22, **22**
Duck Valley, Nevada, **104**
Dutch Antilles, Bonaire town pier, **86**, 87–88, **87**, **88**

E

Ecuador: Cotopaxi National Park, 94, **94**; Guayaquil, **86**, 93, **93**
Elephants: Big Boy, 37–38, **37**, **38**; in India, 53, **53**; in Nepal, 43, **43**
Everglades, Florida, **104**, 109–110, **109**, **110**

F

Fossils, 25, **25**

France, bull fighting in Nimes, **66**, 71–77, **71**, **72**, **73**, **74**, **75**, **76**, **77**

G

Galápagos, **86**; Bartolomé Island, **86**, 96–98, **96**, **97**, **98**; boobies, 4, 99–100, **99**, 127; Daphne Major Island, **86**, 99–100, **99**, **100**; Isabela Island, **86**, 95, **95**; tortoise, 95, **95**, 127

Germany, bazaar in Hamburg, **66**, 78–80, **78**, **79**, **80**

Gorillas in Bwindi Impenetrable Forest, 4, **18**, 26–28, **26**, **27**

Guayaquil, Ecuador, **86**, 93, **93**

H

Hamburg, Germany, bazaar, **66**, 78–80, **78**, **79**, **80**

Hawaii: Curtis and tour of crater, 105–107, **105**, **106**, **107**; Maui, **104**, 105–108; mongoose, 108, **108**

Hawks: on Bartolomé Island, 96–97, **96**, **97**; in Cape May, 111, **111**; in Everglades, 109, **109**; New York Pale Male hawk, 129, **129**

Heron Island, 3, **42**, 51–52, **51**, **52**, 127

Hippos, 33, **33**

Horses: Cotopaxi National Park, Ecuador, 94, **94**; Duck Valley cattle roundup, 120–122, **120**, **121**, **122**; Gypsy horses, 84–85, **84**, **85**; Scrooge, 67–70, **67**, **68**, **69**, 70

Horseshoe crabs, 123–124, **123**, **124**

I

Iguanas, 93, **93**, 97, **97**

Impala, 1, 3, 36

India: Kanha National Park, 49; Kerala and leeches, 54, **54**; Ooty, 53, **53**; Ranthambore, Rajastan, **42**, 47–48; sloth bear in, 50, **50**

Ireland: Ballinasloe and Gypsy horses, **66**, 84–85, **84**, **85**; County Mayo and Scrooge, 67–70, **67**, **68**, **69**, 70

Isabela Island, Galápagos, **86**, 95, **95**

J

Janjin, 64–65, **65**

K

Kalahari, Botswana, **6**; Ebonine, 12–13, **12**, **13**, 14–15, **15**; fire and dancers, 17–18, **17**, **18**; gemsbok, 127; Ngwezumba Molapo Valley, 19; puff adder in, 4, 17; Roger's Camp, **14**; water in, 14, 16, 19

Kangaroo Island, 3

Kanha National Park, India, 49

Kautokeino, Norway, reindeer sled ride, **66**, 81–83, **81**, **82**, **83**

Khao Sok National Park, Thailand, **42**, 55–57, **55**, **56**

Ksors, 25

L

Lavu, 1

Leeches, 54, **54**

Leopards: babysitters, 41, **41**; diet of, 3, 36, **36**

Lions, 39–40, **39**, **40**

M

Macaws: in Brazil, 90–91, **90**, **91**; in Peru, 2, 102–103, **102**, **103**

Mahabil, 47–48, **47**

Masai warriors (Marons), **3**, **8–9**

Maui, Hawaii, **104**, 105–108

Mongolia: Dalanzadgad, **42**, 64–65; Lake Baikel, **42**, 61–63; Three Camel Lodge, 58–59, **85**; Ulaanbaatur, 60

Mongolian tent, **3**

Mongoose, 45, **45**, 108, **108**

Morocco: Rissani, **6**, 21–25, **21**, **23**; Taroudant, 20, **20**

Mushrooms, 34

N

Nairobi, 11, **11**

Nepal and Chitwain National Park, 2, **42**, 43–46, **44**, **45**, **46**

Nevada: Duck Valley, **104**, 120–122, **120**, **121**, **122**; Pyramid Lake, 119, **119**

New Jersey: Brigantine National Wildlife Refuge, 112, **112**; Cape May, **104**, 111, **111**, 123–124, **123**, **124**

New York: Brooklyn, location of, **104**; Brooklyn car service caiman, 126, **126**; Brooklyn pigeons, 115, **115**, 125, **125**; Brooklyn squirrels, 118, **118**; Pale Male hawk, 129, **129**

Nighttime visitors, 58–59, **59**

Nimes, France, **66**, 71–77, **71**, **72**, **73**, **74**, **75**, **76**, **77**

Northwest Territories, 1, 127

Norway: Kautokeino, **66**, 81–83; reindeer in, 4, 81–83, **81**, **82**, **83**

O

Ooty, India, 53, **53**

P

Pennsylvania, Philipsburg roadhouse, **104**, 113–114, **114**

Peru: Cock of the Rock Lodge, 58–59; macaws in, 2, 102–103, **102**, **103**; Manu River Lodge, 59, **86**, 101–103, **101**, **102**, **103**, 130; mercy flight, 130–131, **130**, **131**; spiders in, 1

Philipsburg, Pennsylvania, **104**, 113–114, **113**, **114**

R

Ranthambore, Rajastan, India, **42**, 47–48

Reindeer sled ride, 81–83, **81**, **82**, **83**

Rhinos: in Africa, 7, **7**; in Nepal, 2, 44, **44**

Rissani, Morocco, **6**, 21–25, **21**, **23**

S

Saffron, 20, **20**

Scorpion spider, 1, 101, **101**

Scrooge, 67–70, **67**, **68**, **69**, **70**

Scuba diving, 87–88, **87**, **88**, 98, **98**, 127

Serengeti Plain, **5**, 7–10, **7**, **8–9**, 10

Shaman dance, 4, 61–63, **61**, **62**, **63**

Sloth bear, 46, **46**, 50, **50**

Sycamore Canyon, Arizona, **104**, 116–117, **116**, **117**

T

Taroudant, Morocco, 20, **20**

Tent peg, 21, 24, **24**, 25

Termite mounds, 34

Thailand, **42**, 55–57, **55**, **56**

Throat singing, 60

Tigers, 1, 3

Tortoise, 95, **95**, 127

Travel: how we got started, 5; what we have seen,
 1–4, **1**, **2**, **3**, **4**

Tree Tops Lodge, **6**, 9–10, **11**

Tuareg, 21–24, **21**, **23**

U

Uganda: Bwindi Impenetrable Forest, 4, **6**, 26–28;
 Fort Portal, 29; Murchison Falls, 3, 32; violence
 and war in, 28, 29, 30–32, **31**

Ulaanbaatar, Mongolia, 60

W

Waterfalls, 3

Wolves, 1, 127

Worms, Mopani, 35, **35**

Wrestling, 64–65, **64**, **65**

X

Xakanaxa Camp, Okavango Delta, 33–41, **33**, 128

Z

Zimbabwe, Victoria Falls, 3